HELITA BR SITORUS, ANDY ISMAIL & RIKE SETIAWATI

Building Interactive Business Intelligence Dashboards with Google Looker

Beginner's Practical Book

First published by Asadel Publisher 2024

Copyright © 2024 by Helita Br Sitorus, Andy Ismail & Rike Setiawati

All rights reserved. No part of this publication may be reproduced, stored or transmitted in any form or by any means, electronic, mechanical, photocopying, recording, scanning, or otherwise without written permission from the publisher. It is illegal to copy this book, post it to a website, or distribute it by any other means without permission.

First edition

Advisor: Dr. Rike Setiawati
Proofreading by Andy Ismail, S.Kom., M.M., MTA., MCF., WPPE

This book was professionally typeset on Reedsy.
Find out more at reedsy.com

Contents

Foreword	vii
Introduction	1
II Google Looker Basics	3
2.1 Overview	3
2.2 The Looker Interface	7
Getting Started	7
Key Elements of the Looker Interface	8
2.3 Working with Explores	10
2.4 Understanding Dimensions and Measures	14
Dimensions	14
Measures	15
Using Dimensions and Measures in Explores	15
Practical Example	16
Conclusion	17
III Connecting Data	19
3.1 Supported Data Sources	19
Databases	20
Spreadsheets	20
Cloud Applications	21
APIs	22
3.2 Data Connection Process	22
3.3 Tips for Successful Data Connections	26
3.4 Managing Data Connections	26
3.5 Advanced Data Connection Solutions	27
IV Data Transformation	28
4.1 Why is Data Transformation Necessary?	28

4.2 Performing Data Transformation in Looker	31
4.3 View-Based Data Transformation (Explore)	34
4.4 Model-Based Data Transformation (LookML)	38
Key Features of Model-Based Data Transformation in LookML	38
4.5 Tips for Effective Data Transformation	42
V Data Visualization	**44**
5.1 Types of Data Visualizations	44
Bar Charts	45
Pie Charts	45
Line Charts	46
Maps	46
Tables	47
Gantt Charts	47
Pivot Tables	48
5.2 Choosing the Right Data Visualization	49
5.3 Building Visualizations in Looker	52
5.4 Tips for Effective Data Visualization	56
5.5 Interacting with Visualizations	57
5.6 Dashboards and Data Stories	60
Dashboards	60
Data Stories	63
VI Building Dashboards	**66**
6.1 Define Dashboard Goals	66
Key Questions to Define Dashboard Goals	66
Practical Example: Defining Goals for a Marketing Dashboard	68
6.2 Choose the Right Visualizations	69
Factors to Consider	70
Practical Examples	71
6.3 Layout and Design	72
Principles of Effective Dashboard Layout and Design	73
Steps to Design a Dashboard Layout	74
Practical Example: Designing a Sales Performance Dashboard	76

6.4 Add Filters and Interactivity	77
Adding Filters	77
Adding Interactivity	78
Practical Example: Enhancing a Sales Dashboard	80
6.5 Customize Branding	81
Steps to Customize Branding	81
Practical Example: Customizing a Sales Performance Dashboard	83
6.6 Sharing and Managing Dashboards	84
Sharing Dashboards	84
Managing Dashboards	86
Practical Example: Sharing and Managing a Sales Dashboard	88
6.7 Dashboard Best Practices	90
6.8 Types of Dashboards	90
Types of Dashboards	91
Practical Example: Creating a Sales and Marketing Dashboard	94
VII Sharing Dashboards	96
7.1 Sharing with Colleagues	96
7.2 Sharing with Stakeholders	97
7.3 Sharing with the Public	97
7.4 Tips for Effective Dashboard Sharing	98
VIII Advanced Opportunities with Looker	99
8.1 Advanced Data Analysis	99
8.2 Interactive Data Visualizations	104
8.3 Integrations and Automation	109
Data Integrations	109
8.4 Data Security and Governance	110
8.5 Advanced Use Cases	110
Data Integrations	111
Third-party Tools	112
Workflow Automation	113
Practical Example: Integrating Data and Automating Reports	115
About Author	117

appendix	119
Summary Page Images	120
Draw The Detail Page	127
Trending Page Images	128
Comparison Page Image	130
References	132

Foreword

Praising the presence of Almighty God, for His abundance of mercy and grace, the author was able to complete this book with the title Building an Interactive Business Intelligence Dashboard with Google Looker. This book is presented as a practical guide for users who want to learn how to build informative and effective BI dashboards using the leading Google Looker platform.

In this modern era, data has become an important asset for every organization. The ability to understand and analyze data effectively is key to making the right business decisions. One tool that can help with this is a BI (Business Intelligence) dashboard.

A BI dashboard is a visual tool that presents important data and metrics in an easy-to-understand form. Its function is to help users understand trends, patterns and anomalies in data, so they can make better business decisions.

Google Looker is a popular and easy to use BI platform. With Looker, users can:

- Connect to various data sources, both internal and external
- Perform data transformations to prepare data for visualization
- Build various kinds of interesting and interactive data visualizations, such as charts, tables, and maps
- Design attractive and informative dashboards
- Share dashboards with others and collaborate on data analysis

- This book is designed to help users learn how to build interactive BI dashboards with Google Looker. Here, users will learn various techniques and tips that can be used to build informative and effective dashboards, according to business needs.

Introduction

In today's digital age, data has become an invaluable asset for organizations. The ability to effectively understand and analyze data is a critical factor in achieving business success. Organizations that can leverage data to make informed decisions will have a significant competitive advantage.

However, large amounts of data can often be difficult to comprehend and analyze. Traditional reports filled with tables and lengthy numbers can be tedious and time-consuming to decipher.

This is where Business Intelligence (BI) dashboards come into play. BI dashboards are visual tools that present key insights from data in an easily digestible format. With BI dashboards, users can quickly identify trends, patterns, and anomalies within data, enabling them to make better business decisions.

Google Looker is a popular and user-friendly BI platform. Looker offers a comprehensive suite of features that empowers users to:

- Connect to a wide range of data sources, both internal and external
- Transform data to prepare it for visualization
- Build a variety of engaging and interactive data visualizations, such as charts, tables, and maps
- Design visually appealing and informative dashboards
- Share dashboards with others and collaborate on data analysis

While numerous BI platforms are available, Google Looker possesses several advantages that make it well-suited for organizations of all sizes. Looker's intuitive and user-friendly interface, coupled with its drag-and-drop functionality, allows users to build complex BI dashboards without requiring extensive coding expertise. Additionally, Looker integrates seamlessly with other Google Cloud Platform (GCP) services, making it effortless for users to manage and analyze their data.

This book serves as a practical guide for users seeking to learn how to build interactive BI dashboards with Google Looker. It delves into the fundamental concepts of Google Looker and outlines the steps necessary to construct informative and effective BI dashboards. By following the guidance provided in this book, users will be empowered to harness their data more effectively and make smarter business decisions.

II Google Looker Basics

This chapter introduces you to the core concepts and functionalities of Google Looker, laying the foundation for building effective Business Intelligence (BI) dashboards.

2.1 Overview

- What is Google Looker? Google Looker is a cloud-based BI platform that empowers users to explore, analyze, and visualize data. It simplifies complex data tasks by offering a user-friendly interface and intuitive drag-and-drop functionality.
- Benefits of using Google Looker:
- Centralized data access: Connect to various data sources (databases, spreadsheets, cloud applications) in a single location.
- Data exploration: Utilize Looker's intuitive interface to explore and understand your data through interactive queries.
- Data transformation: Prepare your data for visualization by cleaning, filtering, and aggregating it using LookML (Looker's data modeling language) or the Looker interface.
- Data visualization: Create compelling and interactive visualizations like charts, graphs, and maps to communicate insights effectively.
- Dashboard creation: Design informative dashboards by combining various visualizations and interactive elements for a comprehensive overview of key metrics.

- Collaboration: Share dashboards with colleagues and stakeholders, fostering collaboration and data-driven decision-making.

What is Google Looker?

Google Looker is a cloud-based business intelligence (BI) platform designed to empower users with the ability to explore, analyze, and visualize data seamlessly. This powerful tool simplifies complex data tasks by providing a user-friendly interface complemented by intuitive drag-and-drop functionality, making it accessible even to those who may not have extensive technical expertise. At its core, Google Looker is about turning raw data into actionable insights, helping businesses make informed decisions based on their data.

Benefits of using Google Looker

Centralized Data Access

One of the standout features of Google Looker is its ability to centralize data access. Users can connect to a variety of data sources, including databases, spreadsheets, and cloud applications, all within a single platform. This centralized approach eliminates the need for switching between different tools or platforms, streamlining the data analysis process. Whether the data resides in SQL databases, Google Sheets, or third-party applications like Salesforce, Looker brings it all together, providing a unified view of the data landscape.

Data Exploration

Google Looker excels in data exploration. Its intuitive interface allows users to delve deep into their data through interactive queries. Unlike traditional BI tools that may require extensive SQL knowledge, Looker's interface makes it easy for users to ask questions of their data and get meaningful answers. This capability is crucial for discovering patterns, trends, and insights that may not be immediately obvious. With Looker, users can interact with their data in real-time, adjusting parameters and filters on the fly to uncover new insights.

Data Transformation

Data transformation is a critical step in the data analysis process, and Google Looker offers robust tools to prepare data for visualization. Users can clean, filter, and aggregate their data using LookML (Looker's data modeling language) or through the Looker interface itself. LookML allows for advanced data modeling, defining business logic, and creating reusable data models that can be shared across the organization. This flexibility ensures that data is accurate, consistent, and ready for in-depth analysis and visualization.

Data Visualization

Visualization is where data truly comes to life, and Google Looker provides a suite of tools to create compelling and interactive visualizations. Users can design charts, graphs, maps, and other visual elements to effectively communicate insights. The drag-and-drop functionality simplifies the creation of these visualizations, allowing users to focus on the story they want to tell with their data. Whether it's a bar chart showing sales trends or a map highlighting geographic distribution of customers, Looker's visualization tools make it easy to present data in an engaging and understandable way.

Dashboard Creation

Creating dashboards is another area where Google Looker shines. Dashboards in Looker are more than just a collection of charts; they are interactive, informative, and designed to provide a comprehensive overview of key metrics. Users can combine various visualizations and interactive elements into a single dashboard, tailoring it to meet the specific needs of their audience. These dashboards can be customized with filters, drill-down capabilities, and real-time updates, ensuring that decision-makers always have the most relevant and up-to-date information at their fingertips.

Collaboration

Collaboration is at the heart of Google Looker. Sharing insights and dashboards with colleagues and stakeholders fosters a culture of data-driven decision-making. Looker makes it easy to share dashboards via email, embed them in other applications, or provide access through user permissions. This collaborative approach ensures that everyone in the organization can benefit from the insights generated by Looker, breaking down silos and encouraging a unified approach to data analysis and decision-making.

Additional Features and Integration

Google Looker also offers a range of additional features and integrations that enhance its functionality. For example, Looker integrates seamlessly with Google Cloud services, enabling users to leverage the power of Google BigQuery for large-scale data analysis. Looker's API capabilities allow for the integration of Looker data and insights into other applications and workflows, extending its reach beyond the Looker platform itself. This flexibility makes Looker a versatile tool that can adapt to the unique needs of different organizations.

Security and Governance

Security and data governance are critical considerations for any BI platform, and Google Looker addresses these with robust features. Looker provides fine-grained access controls, ensuring that users only have access to the data they need. This is particularly important for organizations dealing with sensitive or regulated data. Looker's auditing and monitoring capabilities also provide visibility into data access and usage, helping organizations maintain compliance with internal and external data governance policies.

Scalability

As organizations grow, so do their data needs. Google Looker is designed to scale with the organization, handling increasing volumes of data and users without compromising performance. Whether a small business or a large enterprise, Looker's architecture supports scalability, ensuring that users can continue to rely on it as their primary BI tool as their data needs evolve.

Training and Support

To help users get the most out of Looker, Google offers extensive training and support resources. Looker's documentation, online courses, and community forums provide valuable resources for users at all levels. Additionally, Looker's support team is available to assist with technical issues and provide guidance on best practices, ensuring that users can effectively leverage Looker's capabilities.

2.2 The Looker Interface

- Getting started: This section will guide you through the initial setup process, including logging in, navigating the Looker interface, and familiarizing yourself with the layout.
- Key elements: We'll explore the essential components of the Looker interface, such as the Explore bar, navigation pane, data field selection area, and visualization pane.

Google Looker is designed to be user-friendly, with an interface that simplifies the process of data exploration and visualization. In this section, we will guide you through the initial setup process, including logging in, navigating the Looker interface, and familiarizing yourself with its layout. We will also explore the key elements of the Looker interface, such as the Explore bar, navigation pane, data field selection area, and visualization pane.

Getting Started

Initial Setup

To get started with Google Looker, you first need to log in to your Looker account. If you don't have an account yet, you can sign up through your organization or contact Looker for a trial or demo account. Once you have your credentials, follow these steps:

1. **Login**: Visit the Looker login page and enter your username and password.

2. **Authentication**: If your organization uses single sign-on (SSO), you may need to authenticate through your SSO provider.
3. **Welcome Screen**: Upon successful login, you will be greeted with the Looker welcome screen, which may include tutorials and resources to help you get started.

Navigating the Looker Interface

The Looker interface is designed to be intuitive, with a layout that facilitates easy navigation and access to data. Here's a quick overview of the main components:

1. **Explore Bar**: Located at the top of the interface, the Explore bar allows you to search for datasets and start new explorations.
2. **Navigation Pane**: On the left side of the screen, the navigation pane provides access to different sections of Looker, including Explores, dashboards, and settings.
3. **Data Field Selection Area**: This area, typically on the right side of the screen, allows you to select and manipulate data fields for your analysis.
4. **Visualization Pane**: The central part of the interface where your data visualizations will be displayed.

Key Elements of the Looker Interface

Explore Bar

The Explore bar is your starting point for data exploration in Looker. Here, you can search for existing datasets or create new explorations. The search functionality is robust, allowing you to quickly find the data you need by typing keywords or phrases related to your datasets. Once you select a dataset, Looker will open a new Explore page, where you can begin analyzing your data.

Navigation Pane

The navigation pane is a critical part of the Looker interface, providing quick access to various features and sections. Key components of the

II GOOGLE LOOKER BASICS

navigation pane include:

1. **Home**: Your personalized home screen, which may include recent activities, favorite dashboards, and suggested content.
2. **Browse**: Allows you to browse through available Explores, dashboards, and reports within your organization.
3. **Explore**: Direct access to the Explore page, where you can start a new data exploration or open existing ones.
4. **Dashboards**: A list of dashboards that you have created or have access to, which you can open for viewing or editing.
5. **Settings**: Access to your account settings, where you can manage your profile, preferences, and administrative settings.

Data Field Selection Area

The data field selection area is where you define the parameters of your data analysis. It typically includes:

1. **Dimensions**: Categorical fields that you can use to segment your data (e.g., date, product category, region).
2. **Measures**: Quantitative fields that represent metrics (e.g., sales revenue, number of units sold).
3. **Filters**: Options to narrow down your data based on specific criteria (e.g., filtering data to show only the last month's sales).
4. **Pivot**: Allows you to pivot your data to compare multiple dimensions or measures side by side.

By selecting and arranging these fields, you can tailor your data exploration to suit your analysis needs. Looker's drag-and-drop functionality makes it easy to add, remove, or rearrange fields, giving you the flexibility to experiment with different views of your data.

Visualization Pane

The visualization pane is where your data comes to life. This central area of the Looker interface displays the visual representations of your data, such as charts, graphs, and tables. Here are some key features:

1. **Visualization Types**: Looker offers a variety of visualization types, including bar charts, line charts, pie charts, maps, and more. You can switch between different types to find the best way to represent your data.
2. **Customization Options**: Customize your visualizations by adjusting colors, labels, axes, and other settings to enhance clarity and impact.
3. **Interactivity**: Many visualizations in Looker are interactive, allowing you to hover over data points to see details, drill down into more granular data, and apply filters directly from the visualization.
4. **Saving and Sharing**: Once you have created a visualization, you can save it as part of a dashboard, share it with colleagues, or export it for use in other reports or presentations.

2.3 Working with Explores

- What are Explores? Explores are the foundation of data analysis in Looker. They allow you to build queries and explore your data interactively.
- Building Explores: Learn how to navigate different data fields, filter your data based on specific criteria, and aggregate data to uncover trends and patterns.
- Saving and Sharing Explores: Discover how to save your explorations for future reference and share them with colleagues for collaborative analysis.

In Google Looker, Explores are the cornerstone of data analysis. They provide a dynamic environment where users can build queries and interactively explore their data to uncover insights. This section will cover what Explores are, how to build and refine them, and the methods for saving and sharing your explorations for collaborative analysis.

- What are Explores?

Explores are a fundamental feature in Looker that enable users to interact with their data in a meaningful way. Essentially, an Explore is a customizable view of a dataset where you can perform various analytical tasks. Through Explores, you can create queries, filter and aggregate data, and visualize the results—all within an intuitive interface. This interactive approach allows users to dive deep into their data, uncovering trends, patterns, and insights that drive informed decision-making.

- Building Explores

Building Explores in Looker is a straightforward process that involves navigating through data fields, applying filters, and aggregating data. Here's a step-by-step guide on how to build an effective Explore:

Navigating Data Fields

- **Select Your Dataset**: Begin by choosing the dataset you want to explore from the Explore bar. Looker will open a new Explore page with the selected dataset.
- **Dimensions and Measures**: The data field selection area will display available dimensions (categorical data) and measures (quantitative data). Drag and drop these fields into the query area to start building your Explore.
- **Organizing Fields**: Arrange the selected fields in a way that makes sense for your analysis. For instance, you might drag a date dimension to the rows and a sales measure to the columns to analyze sales over time.

Filtering Data

- **Adding Filters**: To narrow down your analysis, apply filters to your

data. Filters can be added by selecting the desired field and specifying the criteria (e.g., filtering sales data to show only the last quarter).
- **Customizing Filters**: Looker allows for complex filtering logic, including multiple filters with AND/OR conditions. This flexibility helps you focus on the most relevant data for your analysis.

Aggregating Data

- **Aggregation Options**: Aggregating data involves summarizing it to uncover trends and patterns. Common aggregation functions include SUM, AVERAGE, COUNT, and MAX/MIN. Apply these functions to your measures to generate meaningful insights.
- **Pivoting Data**: Use the pivot feature to compare different dimensions or measures side by side. For example, you can pivot sales data by product category and region to see how different categories perform across various regions.

Visualization

- **Choosing Visualization Types**: Once your data is prepared, select a visualization type that best represents your analysis. Looker offers a variety of options, including bar charts, line charts, scatter plots, and maps.
- **Customizing Visualizations**: Customize your visualizations by adjusting settings such as colors, labels, and axes. This step ensures that your visual representation is clear and effective in communicating the insights.
- Saving and Sharing Explores

After building an Explore, you may want to save it for future reference or share it with colleagues for collaborative analysis. Looker makes this process easy and efficient.

Saving Explores

II GOOGLE LOOKER BASICS

- **Save As Look**: Once you are satisfied with your Explore, save it as a Look. A Look is a saved query that retains all your settings, filters, and visualizations.
- **Organizing Looks**: Save your Looks in folders for better organization. This practice helps you and your team quickly locate and access specific analyses when needed.

Sharing Explores

- **Sharing Links**: Looker allows you to share Explores via links. You can generate a shareable link and send it to colleagues, giving them access to the same interactive analysis.
- **Embedding and Exporting**: Embed your Explores in other applications or export them as reports in various formats (e.g., PDF, Excel). This versatility ensures that your insights can be shared across different platforms and with a broader audience.
- **User Permissions**: Control who can view or edit your Explores by setting user permissions. This feature ensures that sensitive data is accessible only to authorized users, maintaining data security and integrity.
- Collaboration

Collaboration is a key aspect of data analysis in Looker. By sharing Explores, you can engage in collaborative discussions, refine analyses based on feedback, and ensure that all stakeholders are aligned with the insights derived from the data. Here are some ways to enhance collaboration using Looker:

- **Comments and Annotations**: Add comments or annotations to your Explores to provide context or highlight specific insights. This practice helps colleagues understand the rationale behind certain analyses and fosters a collaborative environment.
- **Version Control**: Looker's version control features allow you to track changes made to Explores, ensuring that you can revert to previous

versions if needed. This capability is particularly useful in collaborative settings where multiple users may be working on the same analysis.
- **Scheduled Reports**: Schedule reports to be automatically generated and distributed at regular intervals. This feature ensures that stakeholders receive timely updates on key metrics without the need for manual intervention.

2.4 Understanding Dimensions and Measures

- Dimensions: Dimensions represent the categories or attributes in your data that act as filters to segment and analyze your data (e.g., customer name, product category, date).
- Measures: Measures represent the quantitative values in your data that you want to analyze and visualize (e.g., sales amount, number of users, click-through rate).
- Using Dimensions and Measures in Explores: We'll delve into how to effectively combine dimensions and measures to build meaningful queries and visualizations.

In Google Looker, dimensions and measures are fundamental elements that allow users to segment and analyze their data effectively. Understanding how to use these components is crucial for building meaningful queries and visualizations. This section will explain what dimensions and measures are, and how to use them in Explores to uncover valuable insights.

Dimensions

Definition: Dimensions represent the categories or attributes in your data that act as filters to segment and analyze your data. They are qualitative and often represent textual or categorical data such as customer names, product categories, and dates.

Examples:

- **Customer Name**: This dimension allows you to segment data by individual customers, helping you analyze customer-specific behaviors and metrics.
- **Product Category**: This dimension categorizes products into groups such as electronics, clothing, or groceries, enabling you to analyze sales or performance by category.
- **Date**: Dates are critical for time-based analysis, allowing you to segment data by day, month, quarter, or year.

Measures

Definition: Measures represent the quantitative values in your data that you want to analyze and visualize. They are numerical and often represent metrics such as sales amounts, the number of users, and click-through rates.

Examples:

- **Sales Amount**: This measure represents the total revenue generated from sales, which can be analyzed to determine performance trends.
- **Number of Users**: This measure indicates the count of users interacting with a product or service, useful for tracking user growth or engagement.
- **Click-Through Rate**: This measure shows the percentage of clicks on a link or advertisement, useful for assessing the effectiveness of marketing campaigns.

Using Dimensions and Measures in Explores

Combining dimensions and measures in Explores is essential for creating insightful queries and visualizations. Here's how to effectively use these components:

Building Queries

1. **Selecting Dimensions**: Start by choosing dimensions that will help you segment your data in meaningful ways. For example, if you want to analyze sales performance, you might select dimensions like Date, Product Category, and Region.
2. **Adding Measures**: Next, add measures that provide the quantitative data you need to analyze. In the sales performance example, you might add measures such as Sales Amount and Number of Transactions.
3. **Filtering Data**: Apply filters to dimensions to focus on specific subsets of your data. For instance, you could filter the Date dimension to analyze sales for the current quarter or filter the Product Category dimension to focus on electronics.

Creating Visualizations

1. **Choosing the Right Visualization Type**: Select a visualization type that best represents the relationship between your dimensions and measures. For time-series data, a line chart may be appropriate, while a bar chart might be better for comparing sales across product categories.
2. **Configuring Visual Elements**: Customize your visualizations by configuring elements such as axes, colors, and labels. This step enhances the clarity and effectiveness of your data presentation.
3. **Interactivity**: Add interactivity to your visualizations by enabling drill-downs and filters. This allows users to explore the data in more detail by clicking on specific data points or adjusting filters.

Practical Example

Let's walk through a practical example to illustrate how to use dimensions and measures in an Explore:
Objective: Analyze quarterly sales performance by product category.

1. **Select Dataset**: Choose the sales dataset from the Explore bar.
2. **Choose Dimensions**:

- Date: Drag this dimension to the query area and group it by quarter.
- Product Category: Add this dimension to segment sales data by product category.

1. **Add Measures**:

- Sales Amount: Add this measure to analyze the total revenue.
- Number of Transactions: Include this measure to understand the volume of sales.

1. **Apply Filters**:

- Filter the Date dimension to focus on the current year.

1. **Build Visualization**:

- Select a bar chart to compare quarterly sales across different product categories.
- Customize the chart by labeling the axes (Quarter, Sales Amount), setting colors for different product categories, and adding data labels for clarity.

1. **Enable Interactivity**:

- Add drill-down functionality to the Product Category dimension, allowing users to click on a category to see detailed monthly sales data within each quarter.

Conclusion

Dimensions and measures are powerful tools in Google Looker that allow you to segment and analyze your data effectively. By understanding how to combine these components in Explores, you can build meaningful queries and visualizations that uncover valuable insights. Whether you are tracking sales performance, analyzing user behavior, or assessing marketing campaigns, mastering the use of dimensions and measures will enhance your ability to make data-driven decisions and communicate your findings clearly.

III Connecting Data

Building effective BI dashboards begins with connecting relevant data. This chapter will guide you through the process of connecting various data sources to Google Looker, unlocking the gateway to powerful data analysis and visualization.

3.1 Supported Data Sources

Google Looker offers flexibility in connecting to a wide range of data sources, including:

- Databases: Connect to relational databases like MySQL, PostgreSQL, and Oracle to access structured data from internal systems.
- Spreadsheets: Import data from Excel or Google Sheets spreadsheets to analyze unstructured or ad-hoc data.
- Cloud Applications: Connect to cloud applications like Salesforce, Google Analytics, and Marketing Cloud to pull marketing and performance data.
- APIs: Utilize APIs to connect to external data sources not naively listed in Looker.

Google Looker provides exceptional flexibility in connecting to a wide array of data sources. This flexibility ensures that users can access and analyze data from various platforms and systems seamlessly. Here, we explore the different types of data sources supported by Looker, including databases, spreadsheets, cloud applications, and APIs.

Databases

Looker supports connections to multiple relational databases, allowing you to access structured data from internal systems. This capability is particularly beneficial for organizations that rely on relational databases for their core business operations. Here are some of the commonly supported databases:

- **MySQL**: A widely-used open-source relational database management system, ideal for handling large volumes of structured data.
- **PostgreSQL**: Known for its robustness and support for advanced data types and indexing, PostgreSQL is another popular choice among businesses.
- **Oracle**: A comprehensive and scalable relational database system that is often used by large enterprises for mission-critical applications.
- **SQL Server**: Microsoft's relational database management system, which is highly integrated with other Microsoft products and services.
- **BigQuery**: Google's highly scalable and fast data warehouse designed for analytics at scale.

Connecting Looker to these databases allows you to leverage SQL-based queries to explore and visualize your data, ensuring that your analyses are grounded in reliable and structured data sources.

Spreadsheets

For analyzing unstructured or ad-hoc data, Looker offers the ability to import data from spreadsheets. This feature is especially useful for businesses that frequently work with data in formats like Excel or Google Sheets.

- **Excel**: Import data from Excel spreadsheets to perform in-depth analysis and create visualizations. This is ideal for scenarios where data collection

and initial analysis have been performed in Excel.
- **Google Sheets**: Directly connect to Google Sheets to access real-time data updates and collaborative features inherent to Google's cloud-based spreadsheet tool.

By integrating spreadsheet data, Looker allows users to combine structured data from databases with more flexible, unstructured data formats, providing a comprehensive view of their data landscape.

Cloud Applications

Looker's ability to connect to cloud applications is a significant advantage for businesses that rely on SaaS (Software as a Service) solutions for their operations. This capability enables seamless data integration from various cloud-based platforms, ensuring that you have a holistic view of your business performance.

- **Salesforce**: Connect to Salesforce to access CRM data, including sales performance, customer interactions, and lead management. This integration helps in analyzing sales pipelines and customer relationships.
- **Google Analytics**: Pull data from Google Analytics to analyze website traffic, user behavior, and marketing campaign performance. This connection is crucial for businesses focused on digital marketing and online presence.
- **Marketing Cloud**: Access data from Marketing Cloud platforms to analyze the effectiveness of email campaigns, social media marketing, and other digital marketing efforts.

By connecting to these cloud applications, Looker enables businesses to leverage the full potential of their marketing and sales data, driving more informed and strategic decisions.

APIs

In addition to the native connectors, Looker supports the use of APIs to connect to external data sources not explicitly listed in its native integrations. This feature ensures that you can still access and analyze data from niche or proprietary systems.

- **Custom APIs**: Utilize RESTful APIs to fetch data from various sources. This is particularly useful for integrating with in-house applications, third-party services, or industry-specific data providers.
- **Web Services**: Connect to web services that provide data feeds in formats such as JSON or XML. This allows you to bring in data from online sources, including news feeds, financial data, and other dynamic content.

Using APIs, Looker can interact with virtually any data source, providing unparalleled flexibility in data integration. This capability ensures that you can incorporate all relevant data into your analyses, regardless of where it originates.

3.2 Data Connection Process

Here are the general steps for connecting a data source to Looker:

1. Create Connection: Access the Looker "Data" menu and select "Connections" to initiate the connection process.
2. Choose Connection Type: Select the type of data source you want to connect to, such as database, spreadsheet, or cloud application.
3. Configure Connection Details: Enter the required connection information, such as database URL, login credentials, and API settings.
4. Verify Connection: Test the connection to ensure accessibility and validity of the source data.
5. Explore and Select Data: Once connected, explore the tables and fields

III CONNECTING DATA

available in your data source.
6. Save Connection: Save your connection for use in building Explores and dashboards.

Connecting a data source to Looker is a crucial step to leverage its powerful data analysis and visualization capabilities. This section outlines the general steps involved in establishing a data connection in Looker, ensuring that you can access and analyze your data effectively.

1. Steps for Connecting a Data Source to Looker
2. **Create Connection**: Access the Looker "Data" menu and select "Connections" to initiate the connection process.
3. **Choose Connection Type**: Select the type of data source you want to connect to, such as a database, spreadsheet, or cloud application.
4. **Configure Connection Details**: Enter the required connection information, such as the database URL, login credentials, and API settings.
5. **Verify Connection**: Test the connection to ensure the accessibility and validity of the source data.
6. **Explore and Select Data**: Once connected, explore the tables and fields available in your data source.
7. **Save Connection**: Save your connection for use in building Explores and dashboards.
8. Detailed Steps

1. Create Connection
To begin the data connection process, follow these steps:

1. **Access the Data Menu**: Log in to your Looker account and navigate to the "Data" menu located in the top navigation bar.
2. **Select Connections**: From the drop-down menu, select "Connections" to open the connections management page.
3. **Initiate Connection**: Click on the "+ New Connection" button to start creating a new data connection.

2. Choose Connection Type

Looker supports various types of data sources. Depending on your specific needs, select the appropriate connection type:

1. **Database**: Choose this option if you are connecting to a relational database like MySQL, PostgreSQL, Oracle, or SQL Server.
2. **Spreadsheet**: Select this option if you are importing data from Excel or Google Sheets.
3. **Cloud Application**: Opt for this if you are connecting to cloud-based services like Salesforce, Google Analytics, or Marketing Cloud.
4. **API**: Use this option for connecting to external data sources via APIs.

3. Configure Connection Details

After selecting the connection type, you need to configure the connection details. The required information may vary based on the type of data source:

1. **Database**:
2. **Database URL**: Enter the URL or IP address of your database server.
3. **Database Name**: Specify the name of the database you want to connect to.
4. **Login Credentials**: Provide the username and password for accessing the database.
5. **Additional Settings**: Include any additional settings such as port numbers, SSL requirements, or connection parameters.
6. **Spreadsheet**:
7. **File Path or URL**: Provide the path or URL to the Excel or Google Sheets file.
8. **Authentication**: Enter the necessary authentication details, such as API keys or OAuth tokens.
9. **Cloud Application**:
10. **API Endpoint**: Specify the API endpoint for the cloud application.
11. **Login Credentials**: Provide the username, password, or API key required for accessing the application.

III CONNECTING DATA

12. **Additional Settings**: Include any other necessary configuration details, such as scope and permissions.
13. **API**:
14. **API URL**: Enter the base URL for the API.
15. **Authentication**: Provide the required authentication credentials, such as API keys, tokens, or OAuth details.
16. **Headers and Parameters**: Specify any additional headers or parameters needed for the API requests.

4. Verify Connection

Testing the connection is crucial to ensure that Looker can successfully connect to your data source. To verify the connection:

1. **Test Connection**: Click on the "Test" button to check if Looker can access the data source using the provided details.
2. **Error Handling**: If the connection test fails, review the error messages, and adjust the connection settings accordingly. Common issues might include incorrect URLs, invalid credentials, or network connectivity problems.
3. **Successful Connection**: Once the connection is successful, you will see a confirmation message indicating that Looker can access the data source.

5. Explore and Select Data

After establishing the connection, you can explore the available data:

1. **Browse Tables and Fields**: Navigate through the list of tables and fields in your data source. Looker will display the schema, allowing you to see the structure of your data.
2. **Select Relevant Data**: Identify and select the tables and fields that are relevant to your analysis. This step ensures that you have access to the necessary data for building Explores and dashboards.

6. Save Connection

Finally, save the connection details for future use:

1. **Save Connection**: Click on the "Save" button to store the connection configuration in Looker.
2. **Naming**: Provide a meaningful name for the connection to easily identify it later.

- **Connection Management**: Looker allows you to manage your saved connections, including editing, deleting, or testing them again as needed.

3.3 Tips for Successful Data Connections

- Identify relevant data sources: Choose data sources that contain the information necessary for your analysis and visualizations.
- Use secure credentials: Ensure you use secure and appropriate credentials to access your data sources.
- Test connections thoroughly: Verify your connections to ensure data accessibility and accuracy.
- Document your connections: Record your connection details for future reference and maintainability.
- Consider data security: Adhere to data security regulations and best practices when connecting and accessing sensitive data.

3.4 Managing Data Connections

Looker provides tools to effectively manage your data connections:

- Monitor connection status: Monitor the status of your connections to

ensure data health and accessibility.
- Update connection details: Update connection details if there are changes to your data sources.
- Delete unused connections: Remove connections that are no longer needed to maintain cleanliness and organization.

3.5 Advanced Data Connection Solutions

Google Looker offers advanced data connection solutions for complex needs:

- Direct Query Connections: Connect directly to databases for real-time analysis and high performance.
- Data Warehouse Connections: Connect to data warehouses for large-scale data analysis.
- Google Cloud Platform (GCP) Services: Integrate with GCP services like BigQuery and Cloud Storage to leverage managed data and data lakes.

IV Data Transformation

Data connected to Google Looker often needs to be transformed to be ready for effective analysis and visualization. This chapter delves into the concepts and techniques of data transformation in Looker, empowering you to manipulate your data and generate more meaningful insights.

4.1 Why is Data Transformation Necessary?

Data transformation plays a crucial role in preparing data for analysis and visualization in Looker. The primary reasons for performing data transformation include:

- Cleaning data: Addressing missing, duplicate, and inconsistent values to ensure data accuracy and reliability.
- Formatting data: Changing data formats to suit analysis and visualization needs, such as converting dates, currencies, and measurement units.
- Calculating new data: Deriving new metrics not directly available in the source data, such as ratios, percentages, and cumulative totals.
- Joining data: Combining data from multiple sources to gain a more holistic understanding of the underlying information.
- Preparing data for visualization: Shaping data into the format required for specific visualization types, such as bar charts, pie charts, and maps.

Data transformation is an essential step in preparing data for analysis and visualization in Looker. This process involves modifying and organizing raw data to ensure it is accurate, consistent, and suitable for generating meaningful insights. The primary reasons for performing data transformation include cleaning data, formatting data, calculating new data, joining data, and preparing data for visualization.

- Reasons for Data Transformation

Cleaning Data

Data cleaning is the process of addressing issues such as missing, duplicate, and inconsistent values. Cleaning data ensures that the information you analyze is accurate and reliable. Without proper cleaning, analyses might yield misleading results due to errors or inconsistencies in the data.

- **Missing Values**: Identify and handle missing values by either filling them with appropriate substitutes (like mean or median values) or excluding them from the analysis if they are not critical.
- **Duplicate Entries**: Remove duplicate records to avoid skewed results and ensure that each data point is unique and accurate.
- **Inconsistent Values**: Standardize inconsistent data entries (e.g., different date formats or varying spellings of the same category) to ensure uniformity across the dataset.

Formatting Data

Data formatting involves changing data formats to suit analysis and visualization needs. Properly formatted data is easier to analyze and visualize, leading to more meaningful insights.

- **Converting Dates**: Transform date formats to a standardized format that Looker can recognize and process correctly.
- **Currencies and Units**: Standardize currencies and measurement units to ensure consistency when performing calculations and comparisons.
- **Text and Numeric Formatting**: Adjust text and numeric data formats

to meet the requirements of specific analyses or visualizations.

Calculating New Data

Often, the raw data available from source systems does not include all the metrics needed for analysis. Data transformation allows you to derive new metrics by performing calculations on existing data.

- **Ratios and Percentages**: Calculate ratios and percentages to understand relationships between different data points, such as conversion rates or growth rates.
- **Cumulative Totals**: Compute cumulative totals to analyze trends over time, such as cumulative sales or running totals.
- **Custom Metrics**: Create custom metrics that are specific to your business needs, such as weighted averages or adjusted revenue figures.

Joining Data

Combining data from multiple sources is crucial for gaining a comprehensive understanding of the underlying information. Data transformation facilitates the joining of disparate datasets, enabling more holistic analyses.

- **Merging Tables**: Combine tables from different databases or data sources to create a unified dataset that includes all relevant information.
- **Creating Relationships**: Establish relationships between different data entities, such as linking customer data with transaction data to analyze customer behavior and purchase patterns.
- **Union and Append**: Perform union or append operations to stack similar datasets on top of each other, useful when dealing with data that spans multiple files or sources.

Preparing Data for Visualization

To create effective visualizations, data needs to be shaped into the format required by the chosen visualization type. Data transformation ensures that the data structure matches the needs of various visualization tools.

- **Aggregating Data**: Summarize data by aggregating it into meaningful categories, such as total sales per month or average customer rating per product.
- **Pivoting Data**: Transform data from a long format to a wide format (or vice versa) to match the requirements of specific visualizations, such as pivot tables or heat maps.
- **Structuring Data**: Rearrange and organize data to highlight key insights and trends, making it easier to communicate findings through visual representations.

4.2 Performing Data Transformation in Looker

Looker provides two primary approaches to data transformation:

1. View-Based Data Transformation (Explore): Data transformation is done directly within Explores while building queries and visualizations. This approach is suitable for simple and quick data transformations.
2. Model-Based Data Transformation (LookML): Data transformation is defined in LookML files, enabling greater control and code re usability. This approach is recommended for complex and repetitive data transformations.

Data transformation in Looker can be performed using two primary approaches: View-Based Data Transformation (Explore) and Model-Based Data Transformation (LookML). Each method has its advantages and is suitable for different types of data transformation needs.

1. View-Based Data Transformation (Explore)

View-Based Data Transformation occurs directly within Explores while building queries and visualizations. This approach is ideal for simple and quick data transformations that can be performed on-the-fly.

Key Features:

1. **Interactive**: Transformations are applied interactively as you build and modify queries in the Explore interface.
2. **User-Friendly**: Designed for users who may not have extensive coding experience. The drag-and-drop interface makes it accessible for business analysts and other non-technical users.
3. **Ad-Hoc Analysis**: Perfect for performing ad-hoc analyses where transformations are needed temporarily or for specific queries.

Common Use Cases:

1. **Filtering Data**: Apply filters to include or exclude specific data points based on certain criteria (e.g., filtering sales data to show only the last quarter).
2. **Aggregating Data**: Summarize data using aggregation functions such as SUM, AVERAGE, COUNT, MAX, and MIN (e.g., calculating total sales or average order value).
3. **Pivoting Data**: Pivot tables to compare different dimensions side-by-side (e.g., comparing sales by product category and region).
4. **Creating Calculated Fields**: Create new fields based on calculations or transformations of existing fields (e.g., calculating profit margin or growth rate).

Example:

To create a calculated field in an Explore:

1. Open the Explore interface and select the dataset you want to work with.
2. Drag and drop the relevant dimensions and measures into the query area.
3. Click on the "Custom Fields" button.

4. Define your calculated field using the available functions and operators (e.g., Sales Amount / Number of Transactions to calculate average sales per transaction).
5. Apply the field to your query and view the results in the visualization pane.
6. Model-Based Data Transformation (LookML)

Model-Based Data Transformation involves defining data transformations in LookML files. LookML (Looker Modeling Language) allows for greater control and reusability of code, making it suitable for complex and repetitive data transformations.

Key Features:

1. **Structured and Reusable**: Transformations are defined in a structured manner within LookML files, enabling code reuse across different Explores and dashboards.
2. **Advanced Capabilities**: Supports complex transformations, data modeling, and business logic that can be reused and maintained centrally.
3. **Collaboration**: LookML allows for version control and collaboration among data engineers and analysts.

Common Use Cases:

1. **Data Modeling**: Define dimensions, measures, and derived fields within LookML views (e.g., creating a unified sales model with consistent metrics across the organization).
2. **Joins and Relationships**: Establish relationships between different tables and data sources (e.g., joining customer data with transaction data).
3. **Advanced Calculations**: Implement complex calculations and logic that need to be reused across multiple reports (e.g., calculating lifetime customer value or cohort analysis).
4. **Data Governance**: Ensure consistent and accurate data definitions by

centralizing transformations in LookML.

Example:
To create a derived measure in LookML:

- Open your LookML project and navigate to the view file where you want to define the transformation.
- Define a new measure within the view

```
measure: average_sales_per_transaction {
type: number
sql: ${total_sales} / ${number_of_transactions} ;;
description: "Average sales amount per transaction"
```

- Save the changes to the LookML file.
- The new measure average_sales_per_transaction is now available for use in Explores and dashboards.

4.3 View-Based Data Transformation (Explore)

View-based data transformation allows you to manipulate data directly within Explores. The available features include:

- Filtering: Filtering data based on specific criteria to focus on relevant data subsets.
- Aggregating: Applying aggregations like SUM, COUNT, and AVERAGE to summarize data.
- Calculating: Calculating new metrics using simple mathematical expressions.
- Formatting: Formatting data such as dates, currencies, and measurement

IV DATA TRANSFORMATION

units.
- Aliasing: Providing more meaningful names for data fields to enhance understanding.

View-based data transformation in Looker enables users to manipulate data directly within Explores, making it accessible and straightforward for quick analysis and visualization. This approach is ideal for performing on-the-fly transformations and adjustments to data without the need for complex coding. The key features available in view-based data transformation include filtering, aggregating, calculating, formatting, and aliasing.

- Features of View-Based Data Transformation

Filtering

Filtering allows you to narrow down your data to focus on specific subsets that are relevant to your analysis. This feature helps in isolating particular data points based on defined criteria.

How to Filter Data:

- Open an Explore and select the dataset you want to work with.
- Drag the field you want to filter by to the "Filters" section.
- Specify the criteria for the filter (e.g., selecting a date range, a specific product category, or a region).
- Apply the filter to update the data displayed in the Explore.

Example: To filter sales data to show only the transactions from the current month:

- Drag the Date field to the Filters section.
- Select "is in the past 30 days" from the filter criteria.
- Apply the filter to see only the sales data for the current month.

Aggregating

Aggregating data involves summarizing it using functions like SUM, COUNT, AVERAGE, MAX, and MIN. Aggregations help in understanding overall trends and patterns in your data.

How to Aggregate Data:

- Select the measure you want to aggregate (e.g., Sales Amount, Number of Transactions).
- Choose the aggregation function you want to apply (e.g., SUM for total sales).
- Drag and drop the measure into the query area, applying the chosen aggregation function.

Example: To calculate the total sales amount:

- Select the Sales Amount measure.
- Choose the SUM function.
- Drag Sales Amount into the query area to display the total sales.

Calculating

Calculating allows you to create new metrics using simple mathematical expressions. This feature is useful for deriving insights that are not directly available in the source data.

How to Calculate New Metrics:

- Click on "Custom Fields" in the Explore interface.
- Define a new calculated field using the available functions and operators (e.g., arithmetic operations, string functions).
- Apply the calculated field to your query.

Example: To calculate the average sales per transaction:

- Click on "Custom Fields".
- Define a new field with the formula Sales Amount / Number of Transac-

tions.
- Apply this field to see the average sales per transaction.

Formatting

Formatting involves adjusting the presentation of data, such as converting dates, currencies, and measurement units. Proper formatting ensures that the data is displayed in a user-friendly and understandable manner.

How to Format Data:

- Select the field you want to format (e.g., Date, Sales Amount).
- Choose the appropriate format (e.g., date format, currency symbol).
- Apply the formatting settings to the field.

Example: To format a date field:

- Select the Date field.
- Choose the desired date format (e.g., YYYY-MM-DD, MM/DD/YYYY).
- Apply the format to display dates in the selected format.

Aliasing

Aliasing allows you to provide more meaningful names for data fields, enhancing the clarity and understanding of the data presented in your reports and dashboards.

How to Alias Data Fields:

- Click on the field name you want to alias in the Explore interface.
- Enter a new, more descriptive name for the field.
- Save the alias to update the field name in the Explore.

Example: To alias a field named cust_id to a more understandable name:

- Click on cust_id.
- Enter the new name Customer ID.

1. Save the alias to update the field name to Customer ID.

4.4 Model-Based Data Transformation (LookML)

Model-based data transformation offers greater flexibility and control through LookML files. LookML uses declarative syntax to define data transformations, including:

- Joining data: Combining data from multiple tables or data sources.
- Filtering data: Filtering data based on complex logic.
- Calculating metrics: Deriving new metrics with intricate calculation logic.
- Formatting data: Formatting data with more granular control.
- Creating new dimensions: Creating new dimensions based on transformation logic.

Model-based data transformation in Looker offers greater flexibility and control through the use of LookML, Looker's data modeling language. LookML employs declarative syntax to define data transformations, enabling advanced data preparation and modeling. This approach is ideal for complex, repetitive transformations and for establishing consistent data definitions across an organization. Key features of LookML include joining data, filtering data, calculating metrics, formatting data, and creating new dimensions.

Key Features of Model-Based Data Transformation in LookML

Joining Data

Joining data involves combining data from multiple tables or data sources to create a unified dataset. LookML allows you to define joins declaratively, specifying how tables are related and how data should be merged.

How to Join Data:

IV DATA TRANSFORMATION

1. Open the LookML view file where you want to define the join.
2. Define the primary view and specify the join with the related table.
3. Specify the join conditions and join type (e.g., left join, inner join).

Example: To join a customers table with an orders table on the customer_id field:

```
view: customers {
dimension: customer_id {
type: number
sql: ${TABLE}.customer_id ;;
}
dimension: customer_name {
type: string
sql: ${TABLE}.customer_name ;;
}

join: orders {
sql_on: ${customers.customer_id} = ${orders.customer_id} ;;
relationship: many_to_one
}
}

view: orders {
dimension: order_id {
type: number
sql: ${TABLE}.order_id ;;
}
dimension: order_date {
type: date
sql: ${TABLE}.order_date ;;
}
}
```

Filtering Data

Filtering data in LookML allows you to apply complex logic to include or exclude specific data points based on defined criteria. This is useful for preparing datasets that meet specific conditions.

How to Filter Data:

1. Define a filter within the LookML view or explore file.
2. Specify the filtering logic using SQL or LookML syntax.

Example: To filter orders to include only those placed in the current year:

```
explore: orders {
view_label: "Filtered Orders"
fields: [order_id, order_date]
filters: {
field: order_date
value: "year(current_date)"
}
}
```

Calculating Metrics

Calculating metrics involves creating new measures based on complex calculation logic. LookML allows you to define these metrics in a reusable manner, ensuring consistency across your analyses.

How to Calculate Metrics:

1. Define a new measure in the LookML view file.
2. Use SQL or LookML functions to specify the calculation logic.

Example: To calculate the average order value:

```
view: orders {
measure: total_sales {
type: sum
sql: ${TABLE}.sale_amount ;;
}
measure: number_of_orders {
type: count
sql: ${TABLE}.order_id ;;
}
```

```
measure: average_order_value {
type: number
sql: ${total_sales} / ${number_of_orders} ;;
description: "Average value of orders"
}
}
```

Formatting Data

Formatting data in LookML provides more granular control over how data is presented. You can specify formats for dates, numbers, and other data types to ensure consistency and readability.

How to Format Data:

1. Define the field you want to format in the LookML view file.
2. Specify the format using LookML syntax.

Example: To format a currency field:

```
dimension: sale_amount {
type: number
sql: ${TABLE}.sale_amount ;;
value_format_name: "currency"
description: "Sale amount in USD"
}
```

Creating New Dimensions

Creating new dimensions in LookML allows you to derive additional fields based on transformation logic. This is useful for generating new categorical data from existing fields.

How to Create New Dimensions:

1. Define a new dimension in the LookML view file.
2. Use SQL or LookML functions to specify the transformation logic.

Example: To create a new dimension categorizing orders by size:

```
dimension: order_size {
type: string
sql:
CASE
WHEN ${total_sales} < 100 THEN 'Small'
WHEN ${total_sales} BETWEEN 100 AND 500 THEN 'Medium'
ELSE 'Large'
END ;;
description: "Order size category based on total sales"
}
```

Model-based data transformation in Looker, facilitated by LookML, provides powerful tools for advanced data preparation and modeling. By leveraging LookML's capabilities to join data, filter data, calculate metrics, format data, and create new dimensions, you can achieve a high degree of flexibility and control over your data transformations. This approach is particularly beneficial for complex and repetitive transformations, ensuring consistency and reusability across your organization's data models. Mastering LookML for data transformation will enable you to build robust, scalable data models that drive accurate and insightful analyses.

4.5 Tips for Effective Data Transformation

- Understand analysis needs: Identify the analysis goals and the data transformations required to achieve them.
- Choose the right transformation method: Use view-based data transformation for simple tasks and model-based data transformation for complex and repetitive tasks.
- Use clear and descriptive names: Name transformed fields and metrics clearly to improve understanding and maintainability.
- Document data transformations: Record data transformation logic for future reference and collaboration.
- Test data transformations thoroughly: Ensure data transformations

IV DATA TRANSFORMATION

produce accurate results that meet analysis needs.

V Data Visualization

Creating effective data visualizations is key to communicating insights and trends clearly from your data. This chapter delves into the concepts and techniques of data visualization in Google Looker, empowering you to craft compelling and informative charts, graphs, and maps.

5.1 Types of Data Visualizations

Google Looker offers a variety of data visualization types to suit different analysis needs:

- Bar Charts: Suitable for comparing metric values across different categories.
- Pie Charts: Used to show the proportions of metric values within a data category.
- Line Charts: Visualize trends and changes in metric values over time.
- Maps: Display geographic data and spatial trends.
- Tables: Present tabular data for detailed analysis.
- Gantt Charts: Illustrate project timelines and workflows.
- Pivot Tables: Summarize and analyze multidimensional data.

Google Looker provides a diverse array of data visualization types to cater to different analytical needs. Each visualization type has its strengths and is suited to specific types of data and analysis objectives. Below, we explore the various data visualization types available in Looker, including their uses and advantages.

Bar Charts

Description: Bar charts are used to compare metric values across different categories. They display data as rectangular bars with lengths proportional to the values they represent.

Use Cases:

- Comparing sales figures across different product categories.
- Analyzing survey responses by demographic groups.
- Evaluating the performance of different marketing campaigns.

Advantages:

- Easy to read and interpret.
- Effective for comparing discrete data points.
- Suitable for both small and large datasets.

Pie Charts

Description: Pie charts show the proportions of metric values within a data category. Each slice of the pie represents a category's contribution to the whole.

Use Cases:

- Displaying the market share of different companies.
- Visualizing the composition of a budget or expenditure.
- Showing the distribution of responses in a survey.

Advantages:

- Provides a clear visual representation of proportions.
- Useful for displaying parts of a whole.
- Easy to understand for a general audience.

Line Charts

Description: Line charts visualize trends and changes in metric values over time. Data points are connected by lines to show how the values change sequentially.

Use Cases:

- Tracking sales performance over multiple quarters.
- Monitoring website traffic trends over time.
- Analyzing stock price movements.

Advantages:

- Ideal for showing trends and patterns over time.
- Helps identify increases, decreases, and fluctuations.
- Suitable for time-series data.

Maps

Description: Maps display geographic data and spatial trends. They can visualize data points, regions, and other spatial information on a map.

Use Cases:

- Mapping customer locations and distribution areas.
- Visualizing regional sales performance.
- Analyzing geographic trends in public health data.

Advantages:

- Provides spatial context to data.
- Effective for identifying geographic patterns and outliers.
- Engaging and visually appealing.

Tables

Description: Tables present tabular data for detailed analysis. They organize data into rows and columns, making it easy to read and compare individual data points.
   Use Cases:

- Displaying detailed financial reports.
- Presenting raw data for in-depth analysis.
- Listing transaction records or inventory details.

Advantages:

- Displays detailed information comprehensively.
- Easy to organize and sort data.
- Suitable for datasets requiring precise values.

Gantt Charts

Description: Gantt charts illustrate project timelines and workflows. They display tasks or activities along a timeline, showing start and end dates and dependencies.
   Use Cases:

- Planning and tracking project schedules.
- Visualizing project timelines and milestones.
- Managing resource allocation and dependencies.

Advantages:

- Provides a clear visual representation of project timelines.
- Helps identify overlapping tasks and potential delays.
- Useful for project management and planning.

Pivot Tables

Description: Pivot tables summarize and analyze multidimensional data. They allow users to rearrange and aggregate data dynamically to extract meaningful insights.

Use Cases:

- Summarizing sales data by region, product, and time period.
- Analyzing financial data across different dimensions.
- Generating summary reports with aggregated metrics.

Advantages:

- Flexible and dynamic data analysis.
- Allows for quick reorganization of data.
- Suitable for complex, multidimensional datasets

Google Looker offers a wide range of data visualization types, each tailored to specific analytical needs and data characteristics. By choosing the appropriate visualization type, users can effectively communicate insights, trends, and patterns in their data. Understanding the strengths and use cases of each visualization type enables you to leverage Looker's capabilities to their fullest, creating compelling and informative visual representations of your data. Whether you are comparing categories, tracking trends over time, mapping geographic data, or analyzing detailed tables, Looker provides the tools needed to turn raw data into actionable insights.

5.2 Choosing the Right Data Visualization

Selecting the right data visualization depends on several factors:

- Data Type: Choose a visualization that suits your data type, such as numeric, categorical, or geographic.
- Analysis Goal: Consider the goal of your analysis, whether it's comparison, trends, or data distribution.
- Audience: Tailor the visualization to your audience, considering their level of expertise and visual preferences.

Selecting the appropriate data visualization is crucial for effectively communicating insights from your data. The right visualization enhances understanding, highlights key trends and patterns, and ensures your audience can easily grasp the information being presented. Here are the primary factors to consider when choosing a data visualization in Google Looker:

- Factors to Consider

Data Type

Different visualizations are suited to different types of data, such as numeric, categorical, or geographic. The nature of your data will guide you in selecting the most appropriate visualization type.

- **Numeric Data**: For numerical data, consider visualizations that highlight distributions, trends, and comparisons.
- **Bar Charts**: Compare discrete numeric values across categories.
- **Line Charts**: Show trends and changes over time.
- **Histograms**: Display the frequency distribution of numeric data.
- **Categorical Data**: For categorical data, use visualizations that emphasize proportions, categories, and relationships.
- **Pie Charts**: Show proportions of categories within a whole.
- **Bar Charts**: Compare values across different categories.

- **Pivot Tables**: Summarize data across multiple categorical dimensions.
- **Geographic Data**: For data with a spatial component, use maps to provide a geographical context.
- **Maps**: Visualize data points or regions on a geographic map.
- **Heat Maps**: Show intensity or frequency of data across geographic areas.

Analysis Goal

The goal of your analysis plays a significant role in determining the best visualization type. Consider whether you aim to compare values, show trends over time, or display data distributions.

- **Comparison**: If your goal is to compare different data points or categories, choose visualizations that highlight differences and similarities.
- **Bar Charts**: Compare metric values across categories.
- **Tables**: Present detailed comparisons in tabular form.
- **Gantt Charts**: Compare project timelines and workflows.
- **Trends**: To show trends and changes over time, select visualizations that effectively illustrate how data evolves.
- **Line Charts**: Display trends and patterns over time.
- **Area Charts**: Emphasize the magnitude of changes over time.
- **Line Graphs with Multiple Series**: Compare trends across different groups or metrics.
- **Distribution**: For displaying the distribution of data, use visualizations that show how data points are spread or clustered.
- **Histograms**: Show the frequency distribution of a single numeric variable.
- **Box Plots**: Display the spread and outliers in a dataset.
- **Scatter Plots**: Visualize the relationship between two numeric variables.

Audience

Understanding your audience is essential for choosing a visualization that effectively communicates your insights. Consider their level of expertise, visual preferences, and how they will use the information.

- **General Audience**: For a broad audience, use simple and intuitive visualizations that are easy to understand.
- **Pie Charts**: Provide a clear representation of proportions.
- **Bar Charts**: Simple and straightforward for comparing categories.
- **Line Charts**: Effective for showing trends over time.
- **Technical Audience**: For a more technical audience, you can use detailed and complex visualizations that provide deeper insights.
- **Pivot Tables**: Allow for in-depth analysis of multidimensional data.
- **Heat Maps**: Show detailed geographic data with intensity variations.
- **Box Plots**: Provide detailed statistical summaries.
- **Executive Audience**: For executives and decision-makers, focus on high-level insights with clear visual impact.
- **Dashboards**: Combine multiple visualizations for a comprehensive overview.
- **Summary Charts**: Highlight key metrics and trends.
- **Infographics**: Present insights in a visually appealing format.
- Practical Examples
- **Example 1: Sales Performance Analysis**
- **Data Type**: Numeric data (sales figures), categorical data (product categories), time series (monthly data).
- **Analysis Goal**: Compare sales performance across product categories and track trends over time.
- **Audience**: Sales team and management.

Recommended Visualizations:

- **Bar Charts**: Compare sales figures across different product categories.
- **Line Charts**: Show monthly sales trends over the past year.
- **Tables**: Present detailed sales figures by product and month.
- **Example 2: Customer Demographics Analysis**
- **Data Type**: Categorical data (age groups, gender), numeric data (number of customers).
- **Analysis Goal**: Understand the distribution of customers across differ-

ent demographic groups.
- **Audience**: Marketing team.

Recommended Visualizations:

- **Pie Charts**: Show the proportion of customers in different age groups and gender.
- **Bar Charts**: Compare the number of customers across various demographic categories.
- **Pivot Tables**: Summarize customer data by age group, gender, and location.
- **Example 3: Geographic Sales Distribution**
- **Data Type**: Geographic data (locations), numeric data (sales figures).
- **Analysis Goal**: Visualize sales distribution across different regions.
- **Audience**: Regional sales managers.

Recommended Visualizations:

- **Maps**: Display sales figures geographically to highlight high-performing regions.
- **Heat Maps**: Show the intensity of sales across different areas.
- **Bar Charts**: Compare sales figures by region.

5.3 Building Visualizations in Looker

Building visualizations in Looker is effortless with its drag-and-drop interface:

1. Select Data Fields: Drag and drop the data fields you want to visualize into the visualization area.
2. Choose Visualization Type: Select the appropriate visualization type

V DATA VISUALIZATION

from the visualization panel.
3. Customize Visualization: Use customization options to modify colors, labels, titles, and other visual elements.
4. Filter and Aggregate Data: Apply filters and aggregations to focus on relevant data subsets.

Building visualizations in Looker is an intuitive process thanks to its user-friendly drag-and-drop interface. This guide will walk you through the steps of creating effective visualizations, from selecting data fields to customizing and refining your visual output.

1. Steps for Building Visualizations in Looker

1. Select Data Fields

The first step in creating a visualization is selecting the data fields you want to visualize. Looker's Explore interface makes this process straightforward:

1. **Open Explore**: Start by opening the Explore interface and selecting the dataset you wish to analyze.
2. **Drag and Drop Fields**: Drag and drop the relevant dimensions and measures into the visualization area. Dimensions are typically used for categories (e.g., dates, product categories), while measures are used for numeric values (e.g., sales amounts, counts).

Example: To visualize monthly sales data:

1. Drag the Date dimension into the visualization area.
2. Drag the Sales Amount measure into the visualization area.

2. Choose Visualization Type

Looker offers a variety of visualization types to best represent your data. Choosing the appropriate visualization type is crucial for effectively communicating your insights.

1. **Access Visualization Panel**: In the Explore interface, click on the visualization panel icon to open the list of available visualization types.
2. **Select Visualization**: Choose the visualization type that best suits your data and analysis goals. Options include bar charts, line charts, pie charts, tables, maps, and more.

Example: To show sales trends over time, select a **Line Chart** from the visualization panel.

3. Customize Visualization

Customization options in Looker allow you to modify various visual elements to enhance readability and impact. You can adjust colors, labels, titles, and other aspects of your visualization.

1. **Open Customization Options**: Click on the settings or customization icon within the visualization panel.
2. **Modify Visual Elements**: Adjust the appearance of your visualization by changing colors, adding or modifying labels, setting titles, and adjusting axes.
3. **Save Customizations**: Once you've customized your visualization to your satisfaction, save your settings.

Example: To customize a line chart:

1. Change the line color to make it more visually appealing.
2. Add a title, such as "Monthly Sales Trends".
3. Adjust the axis labels to ensure they are clear and informative.
4. Filter and Aggregate Data

Applying filters and aggregations helps you focus on the most relevant data subsets and derive meaningful insights from your visualization.

1. **Add Filters**: Drag the fields you want to filter by into the Filters section. Specify the criteria for the filters (e.g., date range, product category).

V DATA VISUALIZATION

2. **Apply Aggregations**: Use aggregation functions like SUM, AVERAGE, COUNT, and others to summarize your data. Aggregations help in condensing large datasets into comprehensible metrics.

Example: To filter and aggregate sales data:

1. Add a filter to include only data from the current year.
2. Apply the SUM aggregation to the Sales Amount measure to show total sales.
3. Practical Example: Creating a Sales Performance Dashboard

Let's create a sales performance dashboard that includes multiple visualizations to provide a comprehensive overview of sales data.

Step 1: Select Data Fields

1. Open the Explore interface and select the sales dataset.
2. Drag Date, Product Category, and Sales Amount into the visualization area.
3. **Step 2: Choose Visualization Types**
4. **Line Chart**: For monthly sales trends.
5. Drag Date to the X-axis.
6. Drag Sales Amount to the Y-axis.
7. Select "Line Chart" from the visualization panel.
8. **Bar Chart**: For sales by product category.
9. Drag Product Category to the X-axis.
10. Drag Sales Amount to the Y-axis.
11. Select "Bar Chart" from the visualization panel.
12. **Step 3: Customize Visualizations**
13. **Line Chart**:
14. Change the line color to blue.
15. Add the title "Monthly Sales Trends".
16. Label the Y-axis as "Sales Amount".
17. **Bar Chart**:

18. Use different colors for each product category.
19. Add the title "Sales by Product Category".
20. Label the X-axis as "Product Category" and Y-axis as "Sales Amount".

Step 4: Filter and Aggregate Data

1. Apply a filter to both visualizations to include only data from the past year.
2. Use the SUM aggregation for Sales Amount to show total sales in both visualizations.

Final Step: Save and Share

1. Save each visualization as a separate Look.
2. Combine the Looks into a dashboard for a comprehensive view.
3. Share the dashboard with relevant stakeholders.

5.4 Tips for Effective Data Visualization

- Use clear and concise charts: Avoid complex and hard-to-understand charts.
- Use consistent and meaningful colors: Choose colors that align with your brand and are easy to distinguish.
- Use clear labels and titles: Label axes and other visual elements clearly.
- Limit the amount of data displayed: Focus on the most important data to avoid clutter.
- Use white space effectively: Use white space to separate visual elements and enhance readability.

V DATA VISUALIZATION

5.5 Interacting with Visualizations

Looker allows interaction with visualizations for deeper analysis:

- Filter data: Click on visual elements to filter data based on that value.
- Explore details: Hover over visual elements to see data details.
- Drill down: Double-click on visual elements to view data at a more granular level.

Google Looker enhances data analysis by allowing users to interact with visualizations for deeper insights. These interactive features include filtering data by clicking on visual elements, exploring details by hovering, and drilling down into data for more granular analysis.

- Interactive Features in Looker

Filter Data
Looker enables users to filter data directly from visualizations, making it easy to focus on specific subsets of data by interacting with visual elements.

- **How to Filter Data:**
- **Click on Visual Elements**: Click on a specific part of the visualization, such as a bar in a bar chart or a segment in a pie chart.
- **Apply Filter**: Looker will automatically filter the data based on the value of the clicked element.
- **Adjust Filters**: You can refine or adjust these filters using the filter pane to meet your analysis needs.

Example: In a bar chart showing sales by region, clicking on the bar representing the "North" region will filter the entire dataset to show only data related to the North region.

Explore Details
Hovering over visual elements in Looker visualizations allows you to

view additional details and data points, providing context and deeper understanding without changing the view.

- **How to Explore Details:**
- **Hover Over Elements**: Move your cursor over different parts of the visualization.
- **View Tooltips**: Looker displays tooltips with detailed information about the data point, such as exact values, percentages, and other relevant metrics.

Example: In a line chart showing monthly sales trends, hovering over a specific data point on the line will display a tooltip with the exact sales figure for that month.

Drill Down

Drilling down allows you to view data at a more granular level by double-clicking on visual elements. This feature is particularly useful for hierarchical data or when you need to analyze data in more detail.

- **How to Drill Down:**
- **Double-Click on Elements**: Double-click on a specific part of the visualization.
- **Navigate to Detailed View**: Looker will display a more detailed view of the data related to the clicked element, often breaking it down further.
- **Explore Further**: Continue drilling down if necessary to navigate through different levels of data granularity.

Example: In a pie chart showing sales by product category, double-clicking on the "Electronics" segment might drill down to show sales by individual products within the Electronics category.

- Practical Application: Creating an Interactive Sales Dashboard

Let's create an interactive sales dashboard that allows users to filter data, explore details, and drill down for deeper analysis.

- **Step 1: Build Visualizations**
- **Sales by Region (Bar Chart)**:
- Drag Region to the X-axis.
- Drag Sales Amount to the Y-axis.
- Select "Bar Chart" from the visualization panel.
- **Monthly Sales Trends (Line Chart)**:
- Drag Date to the X-axis.
- Drag Sales Amount to the Y-axis.
- Select "Line Chart" from the visualization panel.

- **Step 2: Customize Visualizations**
- **Bar Chart**:
- Add title "Sales by Region".
- Label axes appropriately.
- **Line Chart**:
- Add title "Monthly Sales Trends".
- Customize line colors and labels.

- **Step 3: Enable Interactivity**
- **Filter Data**:
- Enable filtering by setting up interactions on the bar chart.
- Users can click on a region to filter the line chart by that region.
- **Explore Details**:
- Ensure tooltips are enabled for both charts.
- Users can hover over bars and line points to see detailed sales figures.
- **Drill Down**:
- Set up drill-down paths for the bar chart.

- Users can double-click on a region to see more detailed data, such as sales by city within the region.

- **Step 4: Combine into a Dashboard**
- **Create Dashboard**:
- Add both the bar chart and line chart to a new dashboard.
- Arrange the visualizations for optimal viewing and interaction.
- **Test Interactions**:
- Click on a bar in the bar chart to filter the line chart.
- Hover over elements to see tooltips.
- Double-click on a bar to drill down into more detailed data.

5.6 Dashboards and Data Stories

- Dashboards: Combine visualizations and text elements into dashboards to provide a comprehensive overview of your data.
- Data Stories: Create compelling data narratives by combining visualizations, text, and commentary to tell the story behind your data.

In Google Looker, dashboards and data stories are powerful tools that allow you to combine visualizations, text elements, and commentary to provide a comprehensive overview of your data and tell compelling data narratives.

Dashboards

Dashboards in Looker are collections of visualizations and text elements that provide a comprehensive overview of your data. They allow you to present multiple pieces of information in a single, consolidated view, making it easier for stakeholders to grasp complex data insights at a glance.

V DATA VISUALIZATION

Creating Dashboards

1. **Create a New Dashboard**:

- Navigate to the Looker menu and select "Dashboards."
- Click on the "Create Dashboard" button to start a new dashboard.

1. **Add Visualizations**:

- Use the drag-and-drop interface to add visualizations to your dashboard.
- Select visualizations from your saved Looks or create new visualizations directly within the dashboard.

1. **Organize Layout**:

- Arrange visualizations in a layout that best suits your analysis needs.
- Resize and move visualizations to optimize the dashboard's readability and visual appeal.

1. **Add Text and Descriptions**:

- Incorporate text elements to provide context and explanations for the visualizations.
- Use text boxes to add titles, subtitles, and descriptive commentary.

1. **Interactive Filters**:

- Add interactive filters to the dashboard, allowing users to dynamically adjust the data displayed in the visualizations.
- Configure filter settings to ensure they apply to the relevant visualizations.

Example: Sales Performance Dashboard

Step 1: Create a New Dashboard

- Name the dashboard "Sales Performance Overview."

Step 2: Add Visualizations

- **Monthly Sales Trends (Line Chart)**: Shows sales trends over the past year.
- **Sales by Region (Bar Chart)**: Compares sales across different regions.
- **Top Products (Pie Chart)**: Displays the proportion of sales by top-selling products.

Step 3: Organize Layout

- Arrange the line chart at the top for a broad view of trends.
- Place the bar chart and pie chart side by side beneath the line chart for detailed comparisons.

Step 4: Add Text and Descriptions

- Add a title: "Sales Performance Overview."
- Include a description box: "This dashboard provides an overview of our sales performance across various regions and top-selling products over the past year."

Step 5: Interactive Filters

- Add a date filter to adjust the time frame.
- Include a region filter to focus on specific regions.

Data Stories

Data stories combine visualizations, text, and commentary to create compelling narratives that explain the insights behind your data. They help communicate the story your data tells in a more engaging and understandable way.

Creating Data Stories

1. **Define the Narrative**:

- Start by identifying the key insights and the story you want to tell with your data.
- Outline the main points and supporting data needed to convey your narrative.

1. **Select Visualizations**:

- Choose visualizations that best illustrate the key points of your data story.
- Ensure each visualization adds value to the narrative and supports the overall message.

1. **Add Commentary and Text**:

- Write commentary that explains the insights shown in each visualization.
- Use text to guide the audience through the data, providing context and highlighting important details.

1. **Incorporate Visual Elements**:

- Use images, icons, and other visual elements to enhance the storytelling aspect.
- Ensure visual elements are relevant and add clarity to the data story.

1. **Structure the Story**:

   - Organize the visualizations and text in a logical flow that builds the narrative.
   - Ensure a clear beginning, middle, and end to your data story.

Example: Quarterly Sales Analysis

Step 1: Define the Narrative

- The story will focus on the sales performance for the past quarter, highlighting key trends, regional differences, and top-performing products.

Step 2: Select Visualizations

- **Quarterly Sales Trends (Line Chart)**: Show overall sales growth.
- **Sales by Region (Map)**: Visualize regional sales performance.
- **Top Products (Bar Chart)**: Highlight best-selling products.

Step 3: Add Commentary and Text

- Introduction: "Our Q2 sales analysis reveals significant growth and regional variations."
- Line Chart Commentary: "Sales increased steadily throughout Q2, with a peak in June."
- Map Commentary: "The East region outperformed other regions, contributing 40% of total sales."
- Bar Chart Commentary: "Product X was the top seller, accounting for 25% of total sales."

Step 4: Incorporate Visual Elements

- Add icons representing regions and products.
- Use color coding to differentiate between high and low sales regions.

Step 5: Structure the Story

- Start with the introduction and overall trends.
- Follow with regional performance and detailed product analysis.
- Conclude with a summary and key takeaways.

VI Building Dashboards

Dashboards are essential tools for visualizing key metrics and trends in a concise and easy-to-understand manner. This chapter delves into the steps and best practices for building effective dashboards in Google Looker.

6.1 Define Dashboard Goals

Before building a dashboard, it's crucial to define its purpose:

- What do you want to convey with this dashboard?
- Who is your target audience?
- What actions do you want your audience to take?

Before building a dashboard in Looker, it is essential to define its goals clearly. This process ensures that the dashboard is focused, effective, and tailored to meet the needs of its intended audience. Here are the key questions to address when defining your dashboard goals:

Key Questions to Define Dashboard Goals

What Do You Want to Convey with This Dashboard?
 Understanding the primary message or insight you want to communicate with your dashboard is critical. This involves identifying the key metrics, trends, and data points that are most important for your analysis.

- **Identify Key Metrics**: Determine the specific metrics that are central to your analysis. For example, if you are building a sales performance dashboard, key metrics might include total sales, sales growth, and top-selling products.
- **Highlight Trends**: Decide on the trends or patterns you want to highlight. This could be sales trends over time, regional sales performance, or customer acquisition rates.
- **Focus on Insights**: Think about the actionable insights you want to provide. These might include identifying areas for improvement, highlighting successful strategies, or predicting future performance.

Example: For a sales performance dashboard, the primary goal might be to convey the overall sales performance, identify high-performing regions, and track sales trends over the past year.

Who Is Your Target Audience?

Knowing your target audience helps you tailor the dashboard's content, design, and complexity to meet their needs and preferences. Different audiences require different types of information and levels of detail.

- **Audience Profile**: Define the profile of your audience. Are they executives, managers, analysts, or operational staff?
- **Information Needs**: Understand what information is most valuable to your audience. Executives might need high-level summaries, while analysts may require detailed data.
- **Expertise Level**: Consider the data literacy and technical expertise of your audience. This will influence the level of detail and complexity of the visualizations you use.

Example: If the target audience is the executive team, the dashboard should provide high-level summaries of sales performance, key trends, and strategic insights, with a focus on clear and concise visualizations.

What Actions Do You Want Your Audience to Take?

Defining the actions you want your audience to take after viewing the dashboard helps ensure that the dashboard is actionable and drives decision-making.

- **Decision-Making**: Identify the decisions that the dashboard should support. For example, should it help managers decide where to allocate resources, or should it guide sales strategies?
- **Actionable Insights**: Ensure that the dashboard provides clear, actionable insights that lead to specific actions. This might include recommendations, alerts, or thresholds that indicate when action is needed.
- **Performance Tracking**: Consider how the dashboard will help track progress towards goals and objectives. Include metrics and KPIs that are aligned with these goals.

Example: For a sales performance dashboard, desired actions might include reallocating resources to high-performing regions, identifying underperforming products to adjust marketing strategies, or setting sales targets for the next quarter based on historical trends.

Practical Example: Defining Goals for a Marketing Dashboard

Step 1: What Do You Want to Convey?

- **Primary Message**: The effectiveness of recent marketing campaigns.
- **Key Metrics**: Campaign reach, engagement rates, conversion rates, and return on investment (ROI).
- **Trends**: Monthly performance of campaigns and comparison between different channels (e.g., social media, email, paid ads).

Step 2: Who Is Your Target Audience?

- **Audience Profile**: Marketing team, including the CMO, campaign managers, and digital marketers.

- **Information Needs**: High-level campaign performance for the CMO, detailed metrics and insights for campaign managers.
- **Expertise Level**: Mixed – high-level summaries for the CMO and detailed analytics for the team.

Step 3: What Actions Do You Want Your Audience to Take?

- **Decision-Making**: Optimize marketing spend, enhance campaign strategies, and allocate resources effectively.
- **Actionable Insights**: Identify successful campaigns, adjust underperforming strategies, and focus on high-ROI channels.
- **Performance Tracking**: Monitor progress towards quarterly marketing goals and KPIs.

Example Summary: The goal of the marketing dashboard is to provide a comprehensive overview of campaign performance, highlight key metrics and trends, and guide strategic decision-making for optimizing marketing efforts.

6.2 Choose the Right Visualizations

Select appropriate visualizations to present your data clearly and concisely. Consider data type, dashboard purpose, and audience preferences.

Selecting the appropriate visualizations for your dashboard is essential to presenting your data clearly and concisely. The right visualization helps convey your message effectively and ensures that your audience can quickly understand and act on the insights provided. Here's how to choose the right visualizations based on data type, dashboard purpose, and audience preferences.

Factors to Consider

Data Type

Different types of data are best represented by specific types of visualizations. Consider whether your data is numeric, categorical, or geographic.

- **Numeric Data**: Best visualized using charts that show trends, distributions, and comparisons.
- **Line Charts**: For showing trends over time.
- **Bar Charts**: For comparing values across categories.
- **Histograms**: For displaying frequency distributions.
- **Scatter Plots**: For showing relationships between two numeric variables.
- **Categorical Data**: Ideal for visualizations that highlight proportions, categories, and comparisons.
- **Pie Charts**: For showing parts of a whole.
- **Bar Charts**: For comparing different categories.
- **Stacked Bar Charts**: For showing the composition of categories.
- **Geographic Data**: Best visualized using maps to provide spatial context.
- **Maps**: For displaying data points or regions on a geographic map.
- **Heat Maps**: For showing intensity or frequency across geographic areas.

Dashboard Purpose

The purpose of your dashboard will guide your choice of visualizations. Consider what you are trying to communicate and what actions you want to drive.

- **Comparison**: Use visualizations that highlight differences and similarities.
- **Bar Charts**: For side-by-side comparisons.
- **Tables**: For detailed, granular comparisons.
- **Trends**: Use visualizations that effectively show changes over time.
- **Line Charts**: For visualizing time series data.
- **Area Charts**: For emphasizing the magnitude of changes over time.

- **Distribution**: Use visualizations that show how data points are spread.
- **Histograms**: For frequency distributions.
- **Box Plots**: For showing the spread and outliers.
- **Composition**: Use visualizations that illustrate parts of a whole.
- **Pie Charts**: For showing proportions.
- **Stacked Bar Charts**: For showing how different components contribute to the total.

Audience Preferences

Tailoring visualizations to your audience's needs and preferences ensures that your dashboard is accessible and engaging.

- **Executives**: Prefer high-level summaries and clear, concise visualizations.
- **Dashboards**: Combine multiple visualizations for a comprehensive overview.
- **KPI Widgets**: Highlight key metrics.
- **Analysts**: Require detailed and interactive visualizations.
- **Tables**: For detailed data views.
- **Pivot Tables**: For multidimensional data analysis.
- **General Audience**: Use simple and intuitive visualizations that are easy to understand.
- **Bar Charts and Pie Charts**: For straightforward comparisons and compositions.
- **Infographics**: For visually appealing and informative presentations.

Practical Examples

Example 1: Sales Performance Dashboard

- **Data Type**: Numeric and categorical (sales figures, product categories).
- **Dashboard Purpose**: Track sales performance, compare regions, and analyze trends.

- **Audience**: Sales managers and executives.

Recommended Visualizations:

- **Line Chart**: For showing monthly sales trends.
- **Bar Chart**: For comparing sales across different regions.
- **Pie Chart**: For displaying the proportion of sales by product category.
- **Tables**: For detailed sales figures.

Example 2: Marketing Campaign Analysis

- **Data Type**: Numeric and categorical (campaign metrics, channels).
- **Dashboard Purpose**: Analyze the effectiveness of marketing campaigns and compare channel performance.
- **Audience**: Marketing team and executives.

Recommended Visualizations:

- **Bar Chart**: For comparing campaign performance across different channels.
- **Line Chart**: For tracking engagement rates over time.
- **Pie Chart**: For showing the distribution of campaign spend.
- **Heat Map**: For visualizing geographic distribution of campaign results

6.3 Layout and Design

Dashboard layouts should be clean, balanced, and easy to navigate. Use visual hierarchy to guide users' eyes to the most important elements.

A well-designed dashboard layout is crucial for ensuring that users can quickly and easily understand the presented data. Effective layouts are clean, balanced, and use visual hierarchy to guide users' attention to the most important elements. Here's how to design a dashboard layout that achieves these goals.

Principles of Effective Dashboard Layout and Design

Clean and Balanced Layout

A clean and balanced layout ensures that the dashboard is visually appealing and not overwhelming. This involves careful arrangement of visual elements, adequate spacing, and consistent styling.

- **Consistency**: Use consistent fonts, colors, and styles across all elements to create a cohesive look.
- **Spacing**: Ensure there is enough white space between visual elements to prevent clutter and improve readability.
- **Alignment**: Align visual elements properly to create a structured and organized layout.

Visual Hierarchy

Visual hierarchy helps guide users' eyes to the most important elements of the dashboard first. This can be achieved through the strategic use of size, color, and positioning.

- **Size**: Larger elements naturally draw more attention. Use larger sizes for the most important metrics and visualizations.
- **Color**: Use color to highlight key information and differentiate between different types of data. Be mindful of using too many colors, which can be distracting.
- **Positioning**: Place the most critical information at the top or in the top-left corner, as users typically start scanning from there.

Steps to Design a Dashboard Layout

1. Define the Structure

Start by defining the overall structure of your dashboard. Consider using a grid layout to ensure alignment and balance.

- **Header**: Include a header that provides the dashboard title and any necessary context or filters.
- **Main Content Area**: Divide the main content area into sections for different types of information (e.g., key metrics, trends, detailed analysis).
- **Footer**: Use the footer for additional information or navigation elements.

Example Layout Structure:

- **Header**: Dashboard title, date range filter.
- **Top Section**: Key performance indicators (KPIs) and summary metrics.
- **Middle Section**: Detailed visualizations such as charts and graphs.
- **Bottom Section**: Tables and additional details.
- **Footer**: Data sources, notes, and navigation links.

2. Organize Visual Elements

Arrange visual elements in a logical order that flows naturally and enhances the user experience.

- **Top-to-Bottom Flow**: Place the most important metrics and visualizations at the top. Users should get a quick overview before diving into details.
- **Grouping**: Group related visualizations together to create a coherent story. For example, place all sales-related metrics in one section.
- **Balance**: Distribute visual elements evenly to avoid overcrowding in any one area.

Example:

1. **Top Section**: Display KPIs such as total sales, total customers, and average order value.
2. **Middle Section**: Use a line chart to show sales trends over time and a bar chart to compare sales by region.
3. **Bottom Section**: Include a table with detailed sales data and a pie chart showing the sales breakdown by product category.

3. Apply Visual Hierarchy

Use visual hierarchy techniques to ensure users focus on the most important information first.

- **Highlight Key Metrics**: Use larger font sizes, bold text, or distinct colors for key metrics.
- **Color Coding**: Apply color coding to differentiate between categories or to highlight critical values (e.g., using red for negative growth).
- **Positioning**: Place essential information in prominent positions, such as the top-left corner or center of the dashboard.

Example:

- **Key Metrics**: Use a larger font and bold text for KPIs at the top of the dashboard.
- **Trend Charts**: Use contrasting colors for lines in a trend chart to make them stand out.
- **Detailed Data**: Position detailed tables and less critical visualizations towards the bottom.

4. Enhance Usability

Ensure the dashboard is user-friendly and interactive to improve the user experience.

- **Interactive Filters**: Add filters that allow users to customize the data displayed (e.g., date range selectors, category filters).

- **Tooltips**: Implement tooltips that provide additional information when users hover over data points.
- **Navigation**: Include clear navigation elements to help users move between different sections or dashboards.

Example:

- **Filters**: Place a date range filter in the header and a region filter next to the relevant visualizations.
- **Tooltips**: Add tooltips to charts to show exact values and additional context.
- **Navigation Links**: Include links in the footer to navigate to related dashboards or reports.

Practical Example: Designing a Sales Performance Dashboard

Step 1: Define the Structure

- **Header**: Title "Sales Performance Dashboard," date range filter.
- **Top Section**: KPIs for total sales, total customers, average order value.
- **Middle Section**: Line chart for sales trends, bar chart for regional sales.
- **Bottom Section**: Table for detailed sales data, pie chart for product category sales.
- **Footer**: Data sources, notes, and links to related dashboards.

Step 2: Organize Visual Elements

- Place KPIs in the top section for a quick overview.
- Arrange the line chart and bar chart in the middle for detailed analysis.
- Position the table and pie chart in the bottom section for additional details.

Step 3: Apply Visual Hierarchy

- Use larger font sizes and bold text for KPIs.
- Apply distinct colors to the line chart and bar chart.
- Place the most important visualizations at the top and center.

Step 4: Enhance Usability

- Add interactive filters for date range and region.
- Implement tooltips for all charts.
- Include navigation links in the footer.

6.4 Add Filters and Interactivity

Utilize filters to allow users to explore data their way. Add interactivity like drill-down and tooltips to provide more information as users interact with the dashboard.

Adding filters and interactivity to your Looker dashboards enhances user experience by allowing users to explore data in ways that are most relevant to them. Filters enable users to focus on specific data subsets, while interactive elements like drill-downs and tooltips provide deeper insights as users interact with the dashboard.

Adding Filters

Filters are essential for creating dynamic and customizable dashboards. They enable users to narrow down data to the specific views that are most relevant to their needs.

Steps to Add Filters

1. **Create Filter Controls**:

- Open your dashboard in edit mode.

- Click on the "Filters" button to add a new filter.
- Select the field you want to filter by, such as date, region, or product category.

1. **Configure Filter Options**:

- Set the filter type (e.g., dropdown, slider, checkbox).
- Define the default filter value if necessary.
- Customize the filter label to make it user-friendly.

1. **Apply Filters to Visualizations**:

- Ensure that each visualization in the dashboard is linked to the filters.
- Configure the filter scope to determine whether it applies to specific visualizations or the entire dashboard.

Example: For a sales performance dashboard:

- Add a date range filter to allow users to select specific periods.
- Include a region filter to enable users to view sales data by geographical area.

Adding Interactivity

Interactivity enhances the user experience by allowing users to explore data in more detail and gain deeper insights.
Drill-Downs
Drill-downs enable users to click on visual elements to view more granular data.
Steps to Add Drill-Downs:

1. **Enable Drill-Downs in Visualizations**:

- Open the visualization settings.
- Enable the drill-down feature.
- Define the hierarchy of data levels (e.g., from country to state to city).

1. **Customize Drill-Down Paths**:

- Specify the fields and dimensions that users can drill down into.
- Ensure that each level provides meaningful and detailed information.

Example: In a bar chart showing sales by region:

- Enable drill-downs to allow users to click on a region and view sales by state.
- Further drill-down from state to city level for more detailed analysis.

Tooltips

Tooltips provide additional information when users hover over data points, helping them understand the context without cluttering the dashboard.

Steps to Add Tooltips:

1. **Configure Tooltips in Visualizations**:

- Open the visualization settings.
- Enable tooltips.
- Customize the content displayed in the tooltip (e.g., exact values, percentages, additional metrics).

1. **Enhance Tooltip Information**:

- Include relevant details such as the data point name, value, and any other contextual information.
- Use formatting options to make the tooltip content clear and readable.

Example: In a line chart showing monthly sales trends:

- Enable tooltips to display the exact sales amount when users hover over a data point.
- Include additional information like percentage growth from the previous month.

Practical Example: Enhancing a Sales Dashboard

Step 1: Add Filters

1. **Date Range Filter**:

- Add a filter for selecting the date range.
- Configure it as a slider to allow users to adjust the period dynamically.

1. **Region Filter**:

- Add a dropdown filter for selecting regions.
- Set the default value to display all regions.

Step 2: Apply Filters to Visualizations

1. **Link Filters to Line Chart**:

- Ensure the date range filter applies to the sales trend line chart.

1. **Link Filters to Bar Chart**:

- Apply the region filter to the sales by region bar chart.

Step 3: Add Drill-Downs

1. **Enable Drill-Down in Bar Chart**:

- Allow users to click on a region to drill down into state-level sales.
- Further enable drilling down from state to city.

Step 4: Add Tooltips

1. **Configure Tooltips in Line Chart**:

- Enable tooltips to show exact sales figures and percentage change.
- Customize tooltip content to include monthly sales and growth rates.

6.5 Customize Branding

Align your dashboard with your company's branding using consistent logos, colors, and fonts.

Customizing your Looker dashboards to align with your company's branding helps create a cohesive and professional appearance. By using consistent logos, colors, and fonts, you can ensure that your dashboards reflect your brand identity and maintain a uniform look across all reports and visualizations.

Steps to Customize Branding

1. Incorporate Company Logo

Adding your company logo to the dashboard enhances brand recognition and gives a professional touch.

Steps to Add Logo:

1. **Upload Logo**: Ensure your company logo is available in a suitable format (e.g., PNG or JPEG).

2. **Add Logo to Dashboard**:

- Open your dashboard in edit mode.
- Drag and drop an image widget to the desired location, typically in the header or top section of the dashboard.
- Upload your company logo to the image widget.

1. **Adjust Size and Position**: Resize and position the logo appropriately to ensure it fits well within the dashboard layout without overshadowing the data visualizations.

Example: Place the company logo in the top-left corner of the dashboard header, ensuring it is visible but not intrusive.

2. Apply Brand Colors

Using your company's brand colors in charts, graphs, and other visual elements ensures consistency with your corporate identity.

Steps to Apply Brand Colors:

1. **Identify Brand Colors**: Gather the hex codes or RGB values of your company's primary and secondary colors.
2. **Customize Visualization Colors**:

- Open the settings for each visualization in your dashboard.
- Apply your brand colors to elements like bars, lines, backgrounds, and text.

1. **Save Color Settings**: Save the color settings to ensure consistency across all visualizations in the dashboard.

Example: If your company's primary color is blue (#0033A0) and secondary color is gray (#CCCCCC):

- Use blue for line charts and bar charts.

- Use gray for backgrounds and secondary elements.

3. Use Consistent Fonts

Applying your company's standard fonts to dashboard text elements, such as titles, labels, and tooltips, helps maintain a cohesive look.

Steps to Use Consistent Fonts:

1. **Identify Standard Fonts**: Determine the fonts used in your company's branding materials.
2. **Customize Font Settings**:

- Open the settings for each text element in your dashboard.
- Apply the standard fonts to titles, labels, and other text elements.

1. **Ensure Readability**: Check that the chosen fonts are legible and appropriately sized for all users.

Example: If your company uses Arial and Helvetica as standard fonts:

- Apply Arial to titles and headers.
- Use Helvetica for labels and smaller text elements.

Practical Example: Customizing a Sales Performance Dashboard

Step 1: Incorporate Company Logo

- **Upload Logo**: Ensure your company logo is in PNG format.
- **Add Logo**: Drag an image widget to the top-left corner of the dashboard header and upload the logo.

Step 2: Apply Brand Colors

- **Primary Color (Blue)**: Use blue (#0033A0) for the main visual elements

like bars in bar charts and lines in line charts.
- **Secondary Color (Gray)**: Use gray (#CCCCCC) for background elements and grid lines.
- **Implementation**: Customize the color settings for each chart in the dashboard.

Step 3: Use Consistent Fonts

- **Title Font (Arial)**: Apply Arial to the dashboard title and main headers.
- **Label Font (Helvetica)**: Use Helvetica for axis labels and tooltips.
- **Implementation**: Adjust the font settings for text elements in each visualization.

6.6 Sharing and Managing Dashboards

Share your dashboards with relevant colleagues and stakeholders. Use Looker's management features to control access and track usage.

Sharing and managing dashboards in Looker ensures that relevant colleagues and stakeholders have access to important data insights while maintaining control over access and usage. Looker provides various features to facilitate sharing, control access, and monitor dashboard usage effectively.

Sharing Dashboards

1. Sharing Options

Looker offers multiple ways to share dashboards with others, making it easy to disseminate important information.

Email Sharing:

- **Steps**:

1. Open the dashboard you want to share.
2. Click on the "Share" button.
3. Select the "Email" option.
4. Enter the email addresses of the recipients.
5. Customize the message and send the email.

- **Use Case**: Ideal for sending snapshots of dashboards to colleagues who prefer receiving updates via email.

Link Sharing:

- **Steps**:

1. Open the dashboard.
2. Click on the "Share" button.
3. Select the "Get Link" option.
4. Copy the generated link and share it via email, chat, or other communication channels.

- **Use Case**: Useful for quickly sharing access with team members who have Looker accounts.

Embedding Dashboards:

- **Steps**:

1. Open the dashboard.
2. Click on the "Share" button.
3. Select the "Embed" option.
4. Copy the embed code and paste it into your website or intranet.

- **Use Case**: Suitable for integrating dashboards into internal portals or websites for broader access.

2. Access Control

Control who can view, edit, or share your dashboards by managing permissions.

Managing Permissions:

- **Steps**:

1. Open the dashboard.
2. Click on the "Settings" or "Permissions" button.
3. Adjust the access settings for different user roles (Viewer, Editor, Admin).
4. Assign specific permissions to individual users or groups.

- **Use Case**: Ensure that only authorized personnel can view or modify sensitive data.

Scheduled Delivery:

- **Steps**:

1. Open the dashboard.
2. Click on the "Schedules" button.
3. Set up a new schedule for delivery.
4. Specify the recipients, delivery frequency, and format (PDF, CSV).

- **Use Case**: Automatically send regular updates to stakeholders, ensuring they stay informed without needing to log into Looker.

Managing Dashboards

1. Version Control

Keep track of changes made to dashboards and revert to previous versions if necessary.

Using Version Control:

VI BUILDING DASHBOARDS

- **Steps**:

1. Enable version control in the dashboard settings.
2. View the version history to see changes made over time.
3. Revert to a previous version if needed.

- **Use Case**: Useful for tracking updates and maintaining a record of changes, especially in collaborative environments.

2. Usage Tracking

Monitor how dashboards are being used to understand engagement and identify potential improvements.

Tracking Dashboard Usage:

- **Steps**:

1. Enable usage tracking in Looker's admin settings.
2. Access usage reports to see who has viewed or interacted with the dashboards.
3. Analyze usage patterns to identify frequently viewed dashboards and those that may need improvement.

- **Use Case**: Helps in understanding the impact of dashboards and optimizing them based on user engagement.

3. Managing Dashboard Organization

Organize dashboards logically to make them easy to find and use.

Creating Folders:

- **Steps**:

1. Navigate to the Looker home page or dashboard directory.
2. Create folders for different departments, projects, or data topics.

3. Move dashboards into the appropriate folders.

- **Use Case**: Improves dashboard organization and accessibility, making it easier for users to find relevant dashboards.

Tagging Dashboards:

- **Steps**:

1. Open the dashboard settings.
2. Add tags to categorize the dashboard (e.g., Sales, Marketing, Finance).
3. Use tags to filter and search for dashboards.

- **Use Case**: Enhances searchability and categorization of dashboards, especially useful in large organizations with many dashboards.

Practical Example: Sharing and Managing a Sales Dashboard

Step 1: Share the Sales Dashboard

1. **Email Sharing**:

- Share the sales performance dashboard with the sales team by email.

1. **Link Sharing**:

- Generate a link and share it with the sales managers via the team communication platform.

1. **Embedding**:

- Embed the dashboard into the company's intranet for easy access by all employees.

Step 2: Control Access

1. **Permissions**:

- Set permissions to ensure only sales managers can edit the dashboard while all sales team members can view it.

1. **Scheduled Delivery**:

- Schedule weekly email reports of the dashboard to be sent to the sales director.

Step 3: Manage the Dashboard

1. **Version Control**:

- Enable version control to track changes made to the dashboard and revert if necessary.

1. **Usage Tracking**:

- Monitor the usage of the sales dashboard to see which metrics are most viewed and make data-driven decisions to optimize the dashboard.

1. **Organize**:

- Place the sales dashboard in the "Sales" folder and tag it with "Performance" and "Monthly Review" for easy access.

6.7 Dashboard Best Practices

- Focus on key metrics: Avoid overwhelming the dashboard with too much data.
- Use consistent visualizations: Employ consistent visual styles and formats throughout the dashboard.
- Consider accessibility: Ensure your dashboard is accessible to users with varying accessibility needs.
- Test and iterate: Gather feedback from users and iterate on your design to enhance dashboard effectiveness.

6.8 Types of Dashboards

- Operational Dashboards: Provide real-time insights into key performance indicators (KPIs) to monitor business health.
- Analytical Dashboards: Dive deeper into data to identify trends and patterns that inform strategic decision-making.
- Executive Dashboards: Present high-level summaries of key business metrics for executives and stakeholders.
- Sales and Marketing Dashboards: Track essential metrics like leads, conversions, and revenue to measure sales and marketing performance.
- Customer Service Dashboards: Offer insights into metrics like customer satisfaction, response times, and churn rates.

Dashboards in Looker can be categorized based on their purpose and the type of insights they provide. Understanding the different types of dashboards can help you design and implement dashboards that meet specific business needs and goals.

VI BUILDING DASHBOARDS

Types of Dashboards

1. Operational Dashboards
Purpose: Provide real-time insights into key performance indicators (KPIs) to monitor the health of daily business operations.
Key Features:

- **Real-Time Data**: Displays up-to-date information to help monitor ongoing activities.
- **Key Metrics**: Focuses on metrics that are crucial for daily operations, such as inventory levels, production rates, and system performance.
- **Alerts and Notifications**: Includes alerts to notify users of any deviations or issues that need immediate attention.

Example: An operational dashboard for a manufacturing company might include real-time data on production output, machine downtime, and inventory levels.
Visualizations:

- Line charts for production rates.
- Gauges for inventory levels.
- Bar charts for system performance metrics.

2. Analytical Dashboards
Purpose: Dive deeper into data to identify trends, patterns, and insights that inform strategic decision-making.
Key Features:

- **Detailed Analysis**: Provides comprehensive data analysis to uncover underlying trends and correlations.
- **Interactive Elements**: Includes filters, drill-downs, and other interactive features to explore data in depth.
- **Advanced Metrics**: Utilizes complex calculations and advanced metrics

to support detailed analysis.

Example: An analytical dashboard for a retail company might analyze sales trends over time, customer purchasing behavior, and product performance.
Visualizations:

- Line charts for sales trends.
- Heat maps for customer purchasing behavior.
- Scatter plots for product performance analysis.

3. Executive Dashboards

Purpose: Present high-level summaries of key business metrics for executives and stakeholders to support strategic oversight and decision-making.

Key Features:

- **High-Level Summaries**: Focuses on top-level metrics and KPIs that are critical for executives.
- **Clear and Concise**: Designed for quick consumption, with straightforward and easily interpretable visualizations.
- **Strategic Insights**: Highlights key insights and trends relevant to business strategy and performance.

Example: An executive dashboard for a tech company might include metrics on revenue growth, market share, and overall company performance.
Visualizations:

- KPI widgets for revenue growth.
- Bar charts for market share comparison.
- Summary tables for overall performance metrics.

4. Sales and Marketing Dashboards

Purpose: Track essential metrics like leads, conversions, and revenue to

measure the performance of sales and marketing efforts.
Key Features:

- **Sales Metrics**: Includes metrics such as sales volume, conversion rates, and revenue.
- **Marketing Performance**: Tracks metrics like lead generation, campaign performance, and ROI.
- **Goal Tracking**: Monitors progress towards sales and marketing goals.

Example: A sales and marketing dashboard might track the number of leads generated, conversion rates, sales by region, and the performance of different marketing campaigns.
Visualizations:

- Funnel charts for lead conversion.
- Line charts for sales trends.
- Bar charts for campaign performance.

5. Customer Service Dashboards
Purpose: Offer insights into metrics like customer satisfaction, response times, and churn rates to improve customer service operations.
Key Features:

- **Customer Satisfaction**: Tracks metrics such as customer satisfaction scores (CSAT) and Net Promoter Scores (NPS).
- **Operational Efficiency**: Monitors response times, resolution times, and the number of open tickets.
- **Retention Metrics**: Analyzes customer churn rates and retention trends.

Example: A customer service dashboard might include metrics on average response time, customer satisfaction scores, and the number of support tickets resolved within a specific timeframe.
Visualizations:

- Gauges for customer satisfaction scores.
- Bar charts for response and resolution times.
- Line charts for churn rate trends.

Practical Example: Creating a Sales and Marketing Dashboard

Step 1: Define the Purpose

- **Goal**: Track the performance of sales and marketing efforts, including leads, conversions, and revenue.

Step 2: Identify Key Metrics

- **Sales Metrics**: Number of leads, conversion rate, total sales, revenue by region.
- **Marketing Metrics**: Campaign performance, cost per lead, return on investment (ROI).

Step 3: Choose Visualizations

- **Funnel Chart**: For lead conversion tracking.
- **Line Chart**: For sales trends over time.
- **Bar Chart**: For comparing campaign performance.
- **KPI Widgets**: For displaying key sales metrics such as total revenue and conversion rate.

Step 4: Design the Layout

- **Top Section**: KPI widgets for key metrics (e.g., total revenue, conversion rate).
- **Middle Section**: Funnel chart for lead conversion.
- **Bottom Section**: Line chart for sales trends and bar chart for campaign performance.

Step 5: Add Interactivity

- **Filters**: Add filters for date range, region, and campaign type to allow users to customize the view.
- **Drill-Downs**: Enable drill-downs on the bar chart to view detailed performance by individual campaigns.

VII Sharing Dashboards

Building compelling and informative dashboards is only half the story. This chapter delves into effective ways to share your dashboards with colleagues, stakeholders, and a wider audience in Google Looker.

7.1 Sharing with Colleagues

- Direct Methods:
- Share Links: Generate unique links for your dashboards and share them with colleagues via email, chat, or other communication tools.
- Embed in Google Drive: Embed your dashboards into Google Drive and share the Drive file with colleagues.
- Embed in Google Sites: Embed your dashboards into Google Sites and share the site with colleagues.
- Indirect Methods:
- Collections: Create dashboard collections and share them with colleagues.
- Spaces: Add dashboards to shared spaces and invite colleagues to collaborate.
- Subscription Filters: Create subscription filters for dashboards and share them with colleagues who want to receive notifications when data updates.

7.2 Sharing with Stakeholders

- Secure Methods:
- Export PDF: Export your dashboard to PDF to share with external stakeholders, maintaining data security.
- Export Image: Export your dashboard to an image (like PNG) to share with external stakeholders, maintaining data security.
- Share Links with Advanced Security: Share dashboard links with advanced security settings, such as passwords and expiration dates.
- Non-Live Methods:
- Scheduled Reports: Create scheduled reports from your dashboards and email them to stakeholders periodically.
- Presentations: Use your dashboards in presentations to convey insights to stakeholders.
- Virtual Meetings: Utilize screen-sharing features in virtual meetings to present your dashboards to stakeholders.

7.3 Sharing with the Public

- Public Publishing:
- Looker Marketplace: Publish your dashboards to the Looker Marketplace for others to discover and use.
- Social Media Platforms: Share screenshots or videos of your dashboards on social media platforms to reach a broader audience.
- Blogs and Websites: Embed your dashboards into your blog or website to share insights with a public audience.
- Important Considerations:
- Data Security: Ensure you follow appropriate data security practices when sharing dashboards publicly.
- Data Privacy: Comply with relevant data privacy regulations when sharing personal data in dashboards.
- Licensing: Consider licensing requirements for reusing or publishing your dashboards.

7.4 Tips for Effective Dashboard Sharing

- Target your audience: Tailor your dashboard sharing approach and presentation style to your audience.
- Provide context: Include contextual information, such as descriptions and notes, to help viewers understand the data.
- Focus on storytelling: Use your dashboard to tell a compelling and easy-to-follow story about your data.
- Encourage interaction: Leverage dashboard interactivity features to encourage your audience to explore the data further.
- Gather feedback: Solicit feedback from users to improve your dashboards over time.

VIII Advanced Opportunities with Looker

Google Looker offers a range of advanced features and capabilities to extend your data analysis and visualization capabilities. This chapter delves into some advanced opportunities you can explore to maximize the power of Looker:

8.1 Advanced Data Analysis

- Custom Data Models: Build complex custom data models to accurately represent your data relationships and support deeper analysis.
- Machine Learning: Leverage Looker's machine learning features to predict trends, identify anomalies, and gain predictive insights from your data.
- SQL Analysis: Utilize Looker SQL to run complex queries, combine data from various sources, and perform advanced data analysis.

Custom Data Models
Custom data models in Looker allow you to build complex representations of your data relationships, enabling deeper and more accurate analysis. These models use Looker Modeling Language (LookML) to define data structures, relationships, and calculations.
Key Features:

- **Complex Joins**: Define complex relationships between tables using LookML, enabling advanced data aggregation and analysis.

- **Derived Tables**: Create derived tables that transform raw data into more meaningful datasets tailored to specific analytical needs.
- **Reusable Components**: Define dimensions, measures, and calculations that can be reused across different analyses and dashboards.

Steps to Build Custom Data Models:

Define Views: Create LookML views to represent each table in your data warehouse. Specify fields, types, and any necessary transformations.

```
view: orders {
dimension: order_id {
type: number
sql: ${TABLE}.order_id ;;
}
dimension: order_date {
type: date
sql: ${TABLE}.order_date ;;
}
measure: total_sales {
type: sum
sql: ${TABLE}.sales_amount ;;
}
}
```

Define Explores: Combine views into explores, defining relationships and joins.

```
explore: orders {
join: customers {
sql_on: ${orders.customer_id} = ${customers.id} ;;
relationship: many_to_one
}
}
```

Advanced Calculations: Add advanced calculations and derived fields to

VIII ADVANCED OPPORTUNITIES WITH LOOKER

support specific analytical needs.

```
dimension: average_order_value {
type: number
sql: ${total_sales} / ${number_of_orders} ;;
}
```

Machine Learning

Looker integrates with machine learning platforms to bring predictive analytics and anomaly detection directly into your data workflows. This enables you to leverage advanced algorithms to gain deeper insights and make data-driven predictions.

Key Features:

- **Predictive Insights**: Use machine learning models to predict future trends and behaviors.
- **Anomaly Detection**: Identify unusual patterns or outliers in your data that may indicate significant events or errors.
- **Integration**: Seamlessly integrate with platforms like Google Cloud AI to run machine learning models on your data.

Steps to Leverage Machine Learning in Looker:

- **Prepare Data**: Ensure your data is clean and well-prepared for machine learning.
- **Integrate ML Models**: Use Looker's integration capabilities to connect with your machine learning platform and import models.

```
measure: predicted_sales {
type: number
sql: PREDICT_SALES(${current_sales}, ${seasonality}, ${trend}) ;;
}
```

- **Visualize Predictions**: Create visualizations to display the predictions and insights generated by your machine learning models.
- Line charts to show predicted vs. actual values.
- Anomaly detection charts to highlight outliers.

SQL Analysis

Looker's SQL capabilities allow you to run complex queries, combine data from multiple sources, and perform advanced data analysis directly within the platform.

Key Features:

- **Complex Queries**: Write and execute SQL queries to perform sophisticated data manipulations and analyses.
- **Data Source Integration**: Combine data from various sources, including databases, cloud services, and spreadsheets, using SQL.
- **Custom Metrics**: Define custom metrics and calculations using SQL for more precise and tailored analysis.

Steps to Perform SQL Analysis in Looker:

- **Write SQL Queries**: Use the SQL Runner or LookML to write and run complex SQL queries

```
SELECT
customers.id,
customers.name,
SUM(orders.sales_amount) AS total_sales
FROM
customers
JOIN
orders ON customers.id = orders.customer_id
GROUP BY
customers.id, customers.name;
```

VIII ADVANCED OPPORTUNITIES WITH LOOKER

- **Combine Data Sources**: Integrate and join data from different sources using SQL.

```
SELECT
a.*,
b.additional_data
FROM
dataset_a AS a
JOIN
dataset_b AS b ON a.id = b.id;
```

- **Create Custom Metrics**: Define and save custom metrics within LookML for use in dashboards and reports.

```
measure: customer_lifetime_value {
type: number
sql: SUM(${total_sales}) / COUNT(${customer_id}) ;;
}
```

Leveraging advanced features in Looker, such as custom data models, machine learning, and SQL analysis, significantly enhances your data analysis capabilities. By building complex data models, integrating predictive analytics, and utilizing powerful SQL queries, you can extract deeper insights, identify trends, and make data-driven decisions with greater confidence. These advanced opportunities empower you to maximize the potential of Looker and drive your business forward with comprehensive and sophisticated data analysis.

8.2 Interactive Data Visualizations

- Custom Visualizations: Create your own custom data visualizations using LookerML, expanding your visualization options to meet specific analysis needs.
- Geospatial Analysis: Use maps and geospatial visualizations to analyze geographic data and uncover spatial trends.
- Cohort Analysis: Create cohort analysis to track the behavior of different user groups over time.

Interactive data visualizations in Looker enhance your ability to explore and understand data by allowing for deeper interaction and customization. This section covers creating custom visualizations, performing geospatial analysis, and conducting cohort analysis to uncover valuable insights.

- Custom Visualizations

Custom visualizations in Looker allow you to create tailored visual representations of your data that go beyond the standard charts and graphs. By leveraging LookerML, you can define custom visualizations that meet specific analysis needs.

Key Features:

- **Customization**: Design visualizations that precisely match your analytical requirements and brand guidelines.
- **Flexibility**: Use JavaScript and other web technologies to create dynamic and interactive visualizations.
- **Integration**: Seamlessly integrate custom visualizations into Looker dashboards.

Steps to Create Custom Visualizations:

- **Define Visualization Requirements**: Determine what data you want

VIII ADVANCED OPPORTUNITIES WITH LOOKER

to visualize and how it should be represented.
- **Create Visualization with LookerML**: Write LookerML code to define the custom visualization.

```
visualization: custom_bar_chart {
label: "Custom Bar Chart"
type: custom
js: {
"type": "d3",
"code": "function drawVisualization() { /* Custom D3 code */ }"
}
options: {
color: {
type: "string",
label: "Bar Color",
default: "blue"
}
}
}
```

- **Integrate and Test**: Integrate the custom visualization into your dashboard and test it to ensure it displays data correctly.
- **Customize and Refine**: Adjust the visualization options and appearance to match your needs.
- Geospatial Analysis

Geospatial analysis in Looker uses maps and other geospatial visualizations to analyze geographic data and uncover spatial trends. This is particularly useful for businesses that operate across multiple locations or need to understand regional patterns.

Key Features:

- **Maps**: Display data points or regions on interactive maps.
- **Heat Maps**: Show intensity or frequency of data across geographic areas.

- **Geospatial Functions**: Use geospatial functions to analyze and manipulate geographic data.

Steps to Perform Geospatial Analysis:

- **Prepare Geographic Data**: Ensure your data includes geographic information such as latitude and longitude or region identifiers.
- **Create Map Visualizations**: Use Looker's built-in map visualization options to display your data.

```
map_layer: my_custom_layer {
type: region
file: "path/to/geojson/file.geojson"
}

explore: my_data {
view: locations {
dimension: region {
type: string
map_layer_name: my_custom_layer
sql: ${TABLE}.region ;;
}
measure: sales {
type: sum
sql: ${TABLE}.sales_amount ;;
}
}
}
```

- **Customize Map Settings**: Adjust map settings such as zoom level, color schemes, and labels to enhance clarity.
- **Analyze Spatial Trends**: Use the map visualizations to identify patterns and trends based on geographic data.
- Cohort Analysis

VIII ADVANCED OPPORTUNITIES WITH LOOKER

Cohort analysis in Looker helps you track the behavior of different user groups over time. This type of analysis is useful for understanding customer retention, user engagement, and other temporal trends.

Key Features:

- **User Group Segmentation**: Segment users into cohorts based on specific criteria, such as signup date or purchase date.
- **Behavior Tracking**: Monitor how different cohorts behave over time.
- **Retention and Churn Analysis**: Analyze retention rates and churn patterns within each cohort.

Steps to Create Cohort Analysis:

- **Define Cohorts**: Segment your users into cohorts based on a relevant event or attribute (e.g., month of signup).
- **Create Cohort Metrics**: Define metrics to track cohort behavior over time (e.g., number of active users, retention rate).

```
dimension_group: signup_date {
type: time
timeframes: [raw, month]
sql: ${TABLE}.signup_date ;;
}

measure: active_users {
type: count
sql: ${TABLE}.user_id ;;
}

measure: retention_rate {
type: number
sql: ${active_users} / NULLIF(${total_users}, 0) ;;
}
```

- **Build Cohort Analysis Visualizations**: Use line charts or heat maps to visualize how cohorts change over time.
- **Interpret and Act**: Analyze the visualizations to identify trends and patterns, and use these insights to inform business decisions.
- Practical Example: Implementing Geospatial and Cohort Analysis

Geospatial Analysis:

- **Prepare Data**:
- Ensure your sales data includes region identifiers (e.g., state, city).
- **Create Map Visualization**:
- Use Looker's map visualization to display sales data by region.
- Customize the map to show sales intensity using a heat map.
- **Analyze Trends**:
- Identify regions with high sales and regions with growth potential.
- Use insights to optimize regional marketing strategies.

Cohort Analysis:

- **Define Cohorts**:
- Segment customers based on their signup month.
- **Create Metrics**:
- Define metrics such as monthly active users and retention rates.
- **Visualize Cohort Behavior**:
- Use a heat map to visualize retention rates across different cohorts.
- **Analyze and Act**:
- Identify trends in user engagement and retention.
- Develop strategies to improve customer retention based on cohort behavior.

8.3 Integrations and Automation

- Data Integrations: Connect Looker to a variety of data sources, including databases, cloud applications, and other analytics platforms.
- Third-party Tools: Utilize Looker's integrations with third-party tools to extend functionality, such as BI tools, CRM tools, and marketing tools.
- Workflow Automation: Create Looker workflows to automate repetitive tasks, such as data processing, report generation, and notifications.

8.3 Integrations and Automation

Google Looker's integration capabilities and automation features significantly extend its functionality and improve efficiency in data analysis and reporting. This section covers connecting Looker to various data sources, utilizing third-party tools, and creating workflows for automation.

Data Integrations

Looker allows you to connect to a wide variety of data sources, including databases, cloud applications, and other analytics platforms. These integrations enable you to centralize your data analysis and leverage diverse datasets for comprehensive insights.

Key Features:

- **Database Connections**: Connect to relational databases such as MySQL, PostgreSQL, Oracle, SQL Server, and more.
- **Cloud Applications**: Integrate with cloud services like Google BigQuery, Snowflake, Redshift, and others.
- **Analytics Platforms**: Connect with other analytics tools to consolidate data and enhance analysis.

Steps to Connect Data Sources:

1. **Access Data Menu**: Navigate to the "Data" menu in Looker.

2. **Create New Connection**:

- Select "Connections" and click on "+ New Connection."
- Choose the type of data source (e.g., database, cloud application).

1. **Enter Connection Details**:

- Provide the necessary connection information, such as database URL, credentials, and any required parameters.
- Test the connection to ensure it is configured correctly.

1. **Save and Use**: Save the connection and start using it to explore and analyze data within Looker.

Example: Connecting to a PostgreSQL database:

8.4 Data Security and Governance

- Data Security: Employ Looker's robust security features to control data access, protect sensitive data, and comply with data privacy regulations.
- Data Governance: Implement sound data governance practices to ensure your data is accurate, consistent, and reliable.
- Auditing and Tracking: Utilize Looker's auditing and tracking features to monitor user activity, track data changes, and ensure compliance.

8.5 Advanced Use Cases

- Business Performance Analysis: Use Looker to track KPIs, measure business performance, and identify opportunities to improve efficiency and profitability.
- Customer Analytics: Gain insights from your customer data to enhance customer experience, drive loyalty, and boost revenue growth.
- Sales and Marketing Analytics: Analyze your sales and marketing data to

optimize campaigns, increase conversions, and improve ROI.
- Operational Analytics: Use Looker to monitor operational processes, identify inefficiencies, and enhance reliability and response times.

8.3 Integrations and Automation

Google Looker's integration capabilities and automation features significantly extend its functionality and improve efficiency in data analysis and reporting. This section covers connecting Looker to various data sources, utilizing third-party tools, and creating workflows for automation.

Data Integrations

Looker allows you to connect to a wide variety of data sources, including databases, cloud applications, and other analytics platforms. These integrations enable you to centralize your data analysis and leverage diverse datasets for comprehensive insights.

Key Features:

- **Database Connections**: Connect to relational databases such as MySQL, PostgreSQL, Oracle, SQL Server, and more.
- **Cloud Applications**: Integrate with cloud services like Google BigQuery, Snowflake, Redshift, and others.
- **Analytics Platforms**: Connect with other analytics tools to consolidate data and enhance analysis.

Steps to Connect Data Sources:

1. **Access Data Menu**: Navigate to the "Data" menu in Looker.
2. **Create New Connection**:

- Select "Connections" and click on "+ New Connection."
- Choose the type of data source (e.g., database, cloud application).

1. **Enter Connection Details**:

- Provide the necessary connection information, such as database URL, credentials, and any required parameters.
- Test the connection to ensure it is configured correctly.

1. **Save and Use**: Save the connection and start using it to explore and analyze data within Looker.

Example: Connecting to a PostgreSQL database:

```
Database: PostgreSQL
Host: mydb.example.com
Port: 5432
Database Name: mydatabase
Username: myusername
Password: mypassword
```

Third-party Tools

Looker integrates with various third-party tools to extend its functionality, making it a versatile component of your data ecosystem. These integrations can enhance business intelligence, customer relationship management, marketing, and more.

Key Features:

- **BI Tools**: Integrate with other business intelligence platforms like Tableau and Power BI for advanced data visualization and analysis.
- **CRM Tools**: Connect with CRM systems like Salesforce to enrich customer data analysis.
- **Marketing Tools**: Integrate with marketing platforms like Google Analytics and HubSpot to analyze marketing performance.

VIII ADVANCED OPPORTUNITIES WITH LOOKER

Steps to Integrate Third-party Tools:

1. **Access Integration Settings**: Navigate to the "Admin" menu and select "Integrations."
2. **Choose Tool**:

- Select the third-party tool you want to integrate with.

1. **Configure Integration**:

- Follow the instructions to connect Looker with the chosen tool. This may involve API keys, authentication, and specific configuration settings.

1. **Validate and Use**: Validate the integration and start using the third-party tool's data and functionalities within Looker.

Example: Integrating Looker with Salesforce:

```
- Go to Admin > Integrations > Salesforce.
- Enter Salesforce API credentials (Client ID, Client Secret, and
Refresh Token).
- Configure data sync settings.
- Validate and test the connection.
```

Workflow Automation

Looker workflows allow you to automate repetitive tasks, such as data processing, report generation, and notifications. Automation streamlines operations, reduces manual effort, and ensures timely data updates and reports.

Key Features:

- **Data Processing**: Automate data cleaning, transformation, and aggrega-

tion tasks.
- **Report Generation**: Schedule automated report generation and distribution to stakeholders.
- **Notifications**: Set up automated alerts and notifications based on data conditions or thresholds.

Steps to Create Workflows:

1. **Identify Automation Needs**: Determine the tasks and processes that can benefit from automation.
2. **Set Up Scheduled Tasks**:

- Navigate to the "Schedules" menu and create a new schedule.
- Define the task, such as data extraction, report generation, or data refresh.
- Specify the frequency and timing of the task (e.g., daily, weekly).

1. **Configure Actions**:

- Define the actions to be performed, such as sending an email, updating a database, or triggering a webhook.
- Customize the content and recipients for reports and notifications.

1. **Activate and Monitor**: Activate the workflow and monitor its execution to ensure it operates correctly.

Example: Automating a weekly sales report:

1. **Set Up Schedule**:

- Go to Schedules > + New Schedule.
- Name: Weekly Sales Report.
- Frequency: Every Monday at 8 AM.

1. **Configure Report**:

- Select the dashboard or report to be generated.
- Specify the format (PDF, Excel) and recipients.

1. **Activate Workflow**:

- Save and activate the schedule.
- Monitor the execution and ensure reports are delivered as expected.

Practical Example: Integrating Data and Automating Reports

Step 1: Connect Data Sources

- **Database Connection**: Connect Looker to a PostgreSQL database containing sales data.
- **Cloud Application**: Integrate with Google BigQuery for additional data analysis.

Step 2: Integrate Third-party Tools

- **CRM Integration**: Connect Looker with Salesforce to enrich customer data.
- **Marketing Integration**: Integrate with Google Analytics to track marketing campaign performance.

Step 3: Create Automated Workflows

- **Automate Data Processing**: Schedule daily data refreshes and transformations.
- **Report Generation**: Set up a weekly schedule to generate and email sales performance reports to the sales team.
- **Notifications**: Configure alerts to notify the marketing team if campaign

performance drops below a certain threshold.

Google Looker's integration and automation capabilities significantly enhance its power and utility, allowing you to connect to a variety of data sources, integrate with third-party tools, and automate workflows. By leveraging these advanced features, you can streamline data processes, enhance analysis, and ensure timely and accurate reporting, ultimately driving better business decisions and efficiency.

About Author

Helita Br Sitorus is a student in the entrepreneurship study program at the Faculty of Economics and Business, Jambi University, class of 2022. Her previous educational background includes attending SMAN Bernas in Riau Province, Pelalawan National Middle School, SD 004 Bukit Agung, and Kindergarten Kuncup Mekar. She was born in Pekanbaru on June 21, 2004, and is currently 20 years old. Helita resides in Mendalo Asri. She has two parents, Nelson Sitorus and Santi, and also has three siblings.

Andy Ismail is an inspiring figure with a rich background in business and literature. As the CEO of PT Asadel Liamsindo Teknologi, he has made significant strides in the Software as a Service (SaaS) industry and Artificial Intelligence (AI) development. His partnerships with prominent global and local technology companies demonstrate his strong commitment to collaboration and innovation.

Dr. Rike Setiawati, born in Jambi on April 3, 1962, has had a remarkable journey marked by dedication and knowledge. She began her academic path by earning a Bachelor's degree in Economics from the Faculty of Economics at Jambi University in 1988. As the seventh child of Sutiem and William Siem Lamsang, Rike did not stop at her undergraduate degree. She pursued further education, obtaining a Master's degree in Management from the Faculty of Economics at Jambi University, graduating with distinction in 2003. Her extraordinary dedication was evident when she earned her Doctorate in Management Science from the Doctoral Program at Universitas Padjadjaran Bandung in 2018.

appendix

Summary Page Images

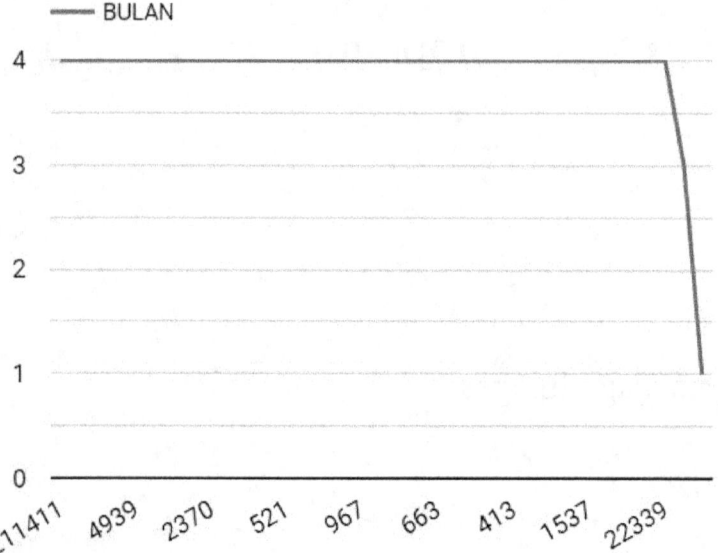

APPENDIX

Total jumlah veteran

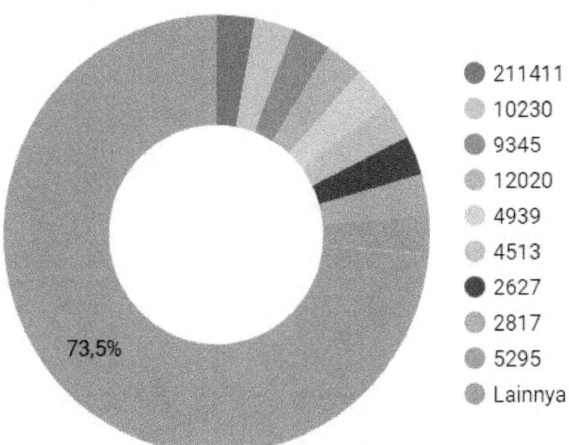

perdamaian, dwikora, dan jumlah

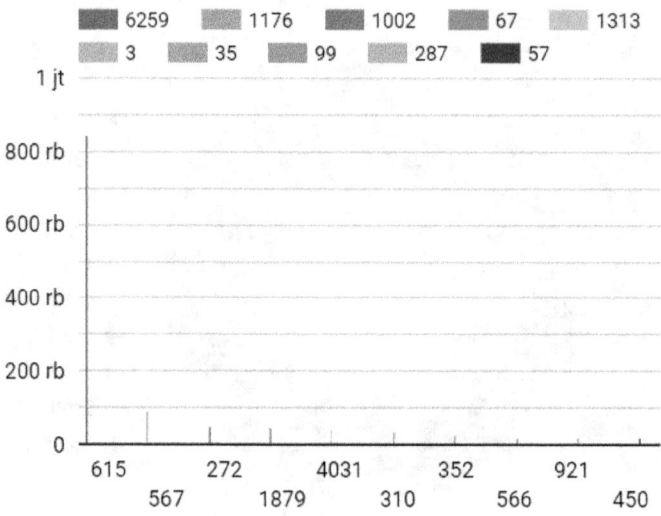

APPENDIX

Jumlah veteran per jenis operasi

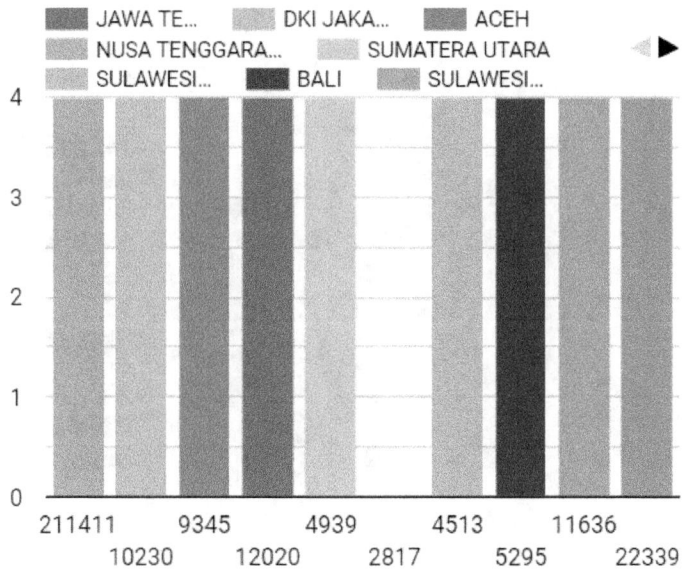

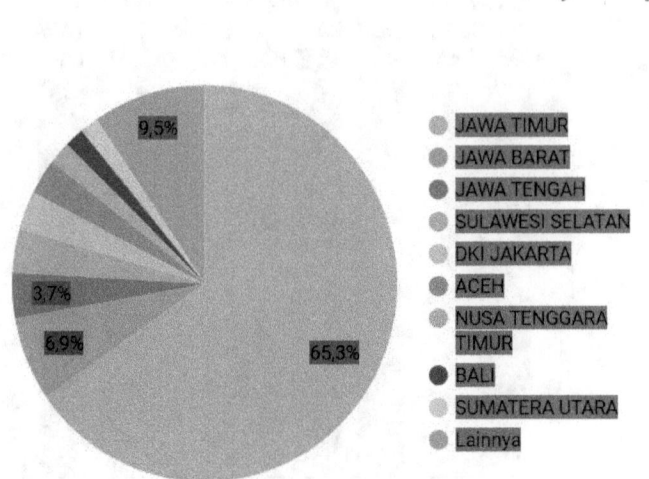

APPENDIX

Mingguan, bulanan, atau tahunan

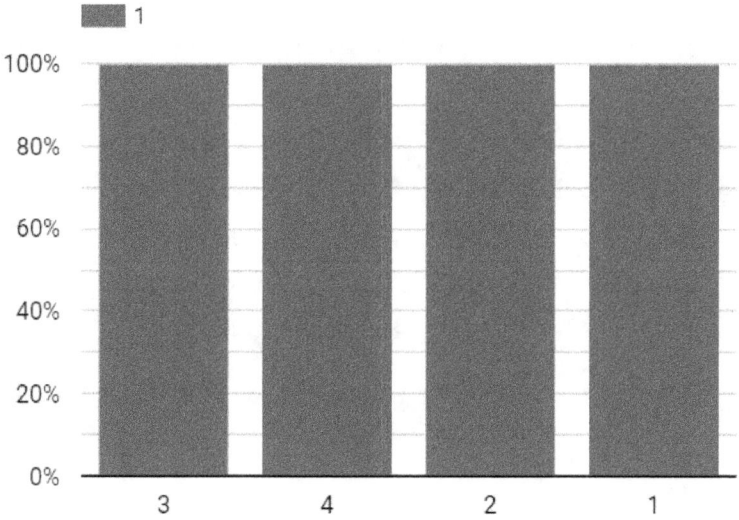

BUILDING INTERACTIVE BUSINESS INTELLIGENCE DASHBOARDS WITH GOOGLE LOOKER

Jumlah veteran per NO, MINGGU, BULAN, TAHUN, PROVINSI, PKRI, TRIKORA, DWIKORA, SEROJA, PERDAMAIAN.

J...	N...	M B...	T...	PR...	P...	TRI...	DWI...	SE...	PERDAM...
1. 8...	3...	1.	4	8.0...	1	1...	28	24	32	136
2. 1...	3...	1.	4	8.0...	1	2...	312	32	0	104
3. 5...	3...	1.	4	8.0...	1	1...	64	12	124	2.040
4. 2...	3...	1.	4	8.0...	1	4...	4	24	196	104
5. 4...	3...	1.	4	8.0...	1	1...	88	844	232	340
6. 5...	3...	1.	4	8.0...	1	9...	64	648	108	508
7. 6...	3...	1.	4	8.0...	1	1...	20	20	400	644
8. 6...	3...	1.	4	8.0...	1	80	1.336	400	52	636
9. 6...	3...	1.	4	8.0...	1	1...	624	48	340	228

1 - 35 / 35 < >

Draw The Detail Page

APPENDIX

Grafik sebar untuk menunjukkan korelasi antara jumlah veteran dan variabel lain.

N...	PROVINSI	PERDAMAI...	BULAN	PKRI	SEROJA
5	DKI JAKARTA	4.031	1	1.791	1.377
39	DKI JAKARTA	4.031	1	1.791	1.377
73	DKI JAKARTA	4.031	1	1.791	1.377
1...	DKI JAKARTA	4.031	1	1.791	1.377
4	SULAWESI SE...	1.879	1	9.227	394
38	SULAWESI SE...	1.879	1	9.227	394
72	SULAWESI SE...	1.879	1	9.227	394
1...	SULAWESI SE...	1.879	1	9.227	394
9	SUMATERA U...	921	1	3.083	403
43	SUMATERA U...	921	1	3.083	403

Trending Page Images

Tren jumlah veteran per provinsi

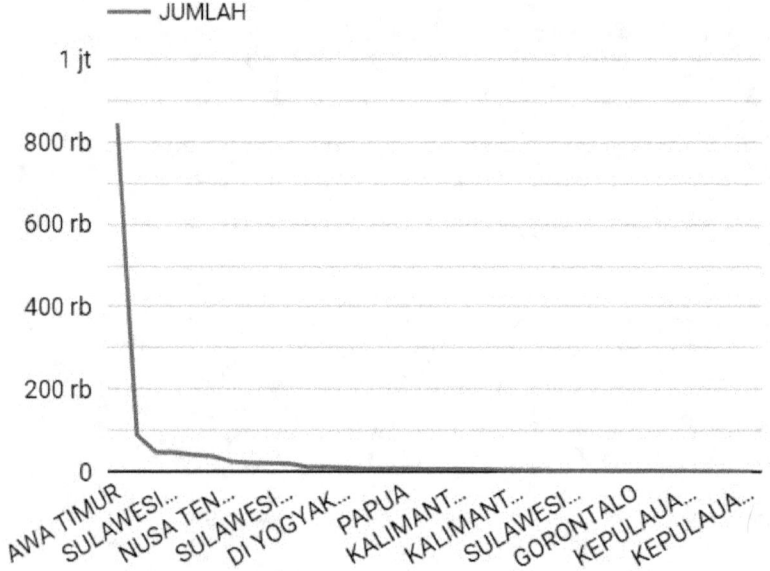

APPENDIX

Mingguan, bulanan, dan tahunan.

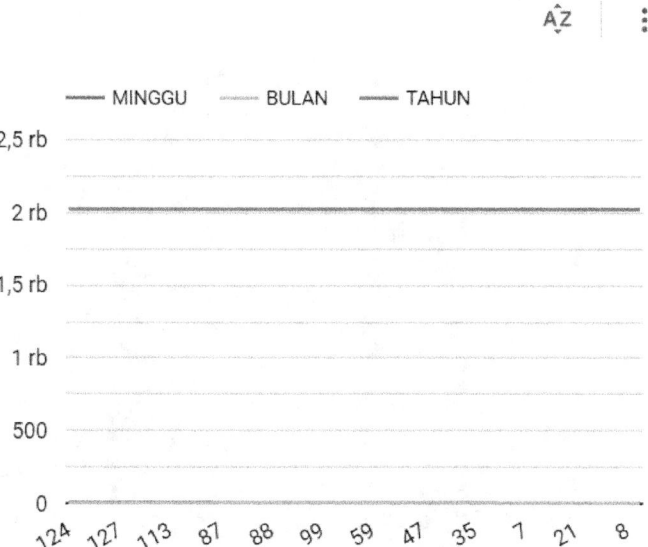

Perbandingan jumlah veteran per provinsi

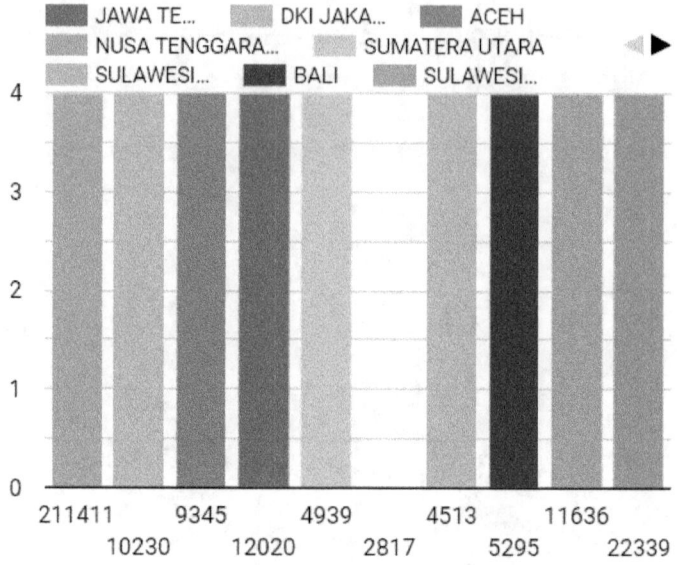

APPENDIX

Perbandingan jumlah veteran Dwikora

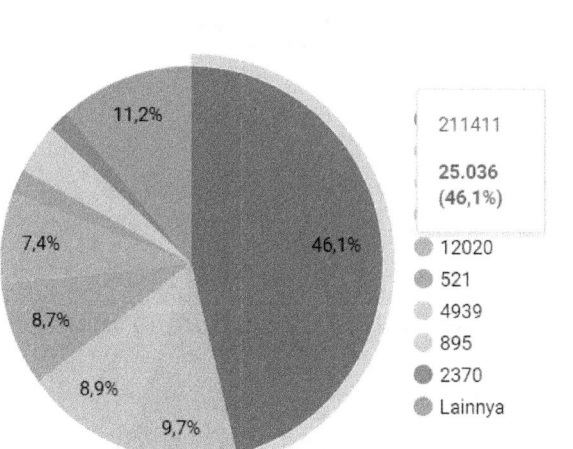

References

Munzner, T. (2014). **Visualization analysis and design**. CRC Press.

Chen, H., Chiang, R. H. L., & Storey, V. C. (2012). Business intelligence and analytics: From big data to big impact. *MIS Quarterly, 36*(4), 1165-1188.

Few, S. (2006). **Information dashboard design: The effective visual communication of data**. O'Reilly Media.

Sources Link

Looker Documentation: https://cloud.google.com/looker/docs
 Looker Help Center: https://support.google.com/looker-studio/?hl=en
 Looker Blog: https://cloud.google.com/looker
 Looker Community: https://cloud.google.com/looker
 Looker Marketplace: https://cloud.google.com/looker/docs/marketplace

Source of Articles and Tutorials

REFERENCES

- **Building Effective Dashboards with Looker:** https://lookerstudio.google.com/visualization
- **Advanced Data Analysis with Looker:** https://cloud.google.com/sql/docs/mysql/looker
- **Creating Custom Visualizations in Looker:** https://cloud.google.com/looker/docs/creating-visualizations
- **Integrating Looker with Third-party Tools:** https://cloud.google.com/looker/docs/api-intro
- **Data Security and Governance in Looker:** https://cloud.google.com/looker/product/security
- **Looker for Business Performance Analysis:** https://cloud.google.com/looker
- **Looker for Customer Analytics:** https://cloud.google.com/looker
- **Looker for Sales and Marketing Analytics:** https://marketplace.looker.com/marketplace/detail/looker-for-google-marketing-platform
- **Looker for Operational Analytics:** https://cloud.google.com/looker

www.ingramcontent.com/pod-product-compliance
Lightning Source LLC
Chambersburg PA
CBHW071927210526
45479CB00002B/590